T0360610

Deconstructing Human Development

This book provides a critical deconstruction of the human development framework promoted by the United Nations Development Programme (UNDP) since 1990. Taking the Human Development Reports of the UNDP as its starting point for reflection, this book investigates the construction of this framework as well as its political function since the end of the Cold War. The book argues that the UNDP's discourse on development relies on essentialist philosophical, cultural, and political assumptions dating back to the 19th century and concludes that these assumptions – also present in the MDGs and SDGs – impede a full grasp of the complex and multi-layered global problems of the current world. Whilst development critiques traditionally relied on liberal, Marxist or Foucauldian theoretical frameworks and focused on epistemological or political economy issues, this book draws on the post-foundational and post-structuralist work of Ernesto Laclau and Jacques Derrida and proposes an ontological and relational reading of development discourses that both complements and further develops the insights of previous critiques. This book is key reading for advanced students and researchers of Critical Development Studies, Political Science, the UN, and Sustainable Development.

Juan Telleria is Assistant Professor in the Department of Philosophy and Researcher at the Hegoa Institute for International Cooperation and Development Studies, University of the Basque Country UPV/EHU, Spain.

Routledge Critical Development Studies
Series Editors

Henry Veltmeyer is co-chair of the Critical Development Studies (CDS) network, Research Professor at Universidad Autónoma de Zacatecas, Mexico, and Professor Emeritus at Saint Mary's University, Canada

Paul Bowles is Professor of Economics and International Studies at UNBC, Canada

Elisa van Wayenberge is Lecturer in Economics at SOAS University of London, UK

The global crisis, coming at the end of three decades of uneven capitalist development and neoliberal globalization that have devastated the economies and societies of people across the world, especially in the developing societies of the global south, cries out for a more critical, proactive approach to the study of international development. The challenge of creating and disseminating such an approach, to provide the study of international development with a critical edge, is the project of a global network of activist development scholars concerned and engaged in using their research and writings to help effect transformative social change that might lead to a better world.

Deconstructing Human Development

From the Washington Consensus to the 2030 Agenda

Juan Telleria

Routledge
Taylor & Francis Group

LONDON AND NEW YORK

First published 2021
by Routledge
2 Park Square, Milton Park, Abingdon, Oxon OX14 4RN

and by Routledge
52 Vanderbilt Avenue, New York, NY 10017

Routledge is an imprint of the Taylor & Francis Group, an informa business

© 2021 Juan Telleria

British Library Cataloguing in Publication Data
A catalogue record for this book is available from the British Library

Library of Congress Cataloging-in-Publication Data
A catalog record has been requested for this book

ISBN: 978-0-367-48956-4 (hbk)
ISBN: 978-1-003-04365-2 (ebk)

Typeset in Times New Roman
by Taylor & Francis Books

To Gemma

Contents

Illustrations

Figures

Box

Acknowledgements

Thanks to Gemma, to my family and to my closest friends for making my life so nice. Thanks also to my friends and colleagues in the Philosophy Department and in the Hegoa Institute for International Cooperation and Development Studies of the University of the Basque Country (UPV/EHU), in the Government Department of the University of Essex (England), and in the Department for Development and Postcolonial Studies of the University of Kassel (Germany) for creating the critical academic environment that stimulated the research in this book.

Introduction
The endless quest

Since Reason gradually replaced God in the search for truth, the cultural, political and academic history of the West has focused on the relentless quest for a better world on earth, and the constant confirmation that such a world is elusive and unreachable. The reality we wanted to conquer and transform seems to be indomitable. There is no need to go back far in history to find examples of this never-ending struggle. The United Nations (UN) was created in 1945 to avoid war, reaffirm human rights and dignity, promote social progress and justice, and ensure security and peace – as stated in the preamble of its charter (UN, 1945: Preamble). Seventy years later, the UN's 2030 Agenda for Sustainable Development describes the world in terms of poverty, lack of dignity, global health threats, violent extremism and terrorism, environmental degradation and climatic change, gender inequality, unemployment, war and spiralling conflicts (UN, 2015: paragraph 14). Nevertheless, the agenda insists that we can 'transform our world'.

In *Emancipation(s)* (1996), Ernesto Laclau reflects on this endless historical quest for a better world, and poses it in terms of universalism and particularism. He asks: 'are the relations between universalism and particularism simple relations of mutual exclusion?' (Laclau, 1996: 22). To deconstruct this binary opposition – universalism/particularism – he goes back to ancient Greece and explains that the founders of the Western philosophical tradition established a clear dividing line between particularity and universality. On one side of this line, the universal was understood as the realm of perfection, truth and absoluteness, which could be reached exclusively through reason; on the other side, the particular was conceptualized as its opposite – imperfect, ephemeral and changeable. On the basis of this dualism, it was assumed that 'the particular can only *corrupt* the universal' (Laclau, 1996: 22). Many centuries later, Laclau continues, Christianity inherited this question, but solved it in a different way. God, through his incarnation and revelation, became the only and absolute mediator between the universal truth and the particular people. He explains:

> A subtle logic destinated to have a profound influence in our intellectual tradition was started in this way: that of the *privileged agent of history*, the agent whose particular body was the expression of a universality transcending it. (...) European culture was a particular one, and at the same time the expression (...) of universal human essence.
>
> (Laclau, 1996: 23–24)

Laclau explains that, once Reason replaced God as the guarantor of truth, Western culture presented itself as the privileged mediator between the universal and the particular. And the history of the West turned into an endless quest of spreading the European (universal) truth. Laclau concludes:

> The various forms of Eurocentrism are nothing but the distant historical effects of the logic of incarnation. (...) European imperialist expansion had to be presented in terms of a universal civilizing function, modernization and so forth. The resistances of other cultures were, as a result, presented not as struggles between particular identities and cultures, but as part of an all-embracing and epochal struggle between universality and particularisms – the notion of peoples without history expressing precisely their incapacity to represent the universal.
>
> (Laclau, 1996: 23–24)

During the same period that Laclau was writing these lines (these insights come from a 1991 symposium in the City University of New York), several critical development researchers extracted similar conclusions, including Wolfgang Sachs et al. in *The Development Dictionary* (1992), Arturo Escobar in *Encountering Development* (1995), and Gilbert Rist in *The History of Development* (1996). It was the beginning of post-development. Strongly influenced by the work of Michel Foucault, this perspective posed its critique in terms of particularism and universalism. To expose the Foucauldian knowledge-power dynamics within development practices, post-development denounced the West for granting itself the role of *the universal subject* – the only epistemological perspective that could achieve truth and explain reality in a transparent, pure and objective way. To overcome the logics that shaped, sustained and reproduced the power relations of the modern, industrial and capitalist era, post-development (1) advocated the rejection of development logics, and instead called for alternatives to development (Ziai, 2017b: 2547–2548); and (2) championed *the valorization of alternative subjectivities* and emphasized the need for plural epistemological perspectives – the pluriverse (Escobar, 2018, 2020; Kothari et al., 2019). Overall, this perspective strongly motivated a generation of researchers – including myself – to critically engage with development discourses and, although it was not always acknowledged as such, exerted considerable influence on mainstream development studies (Ziai, 2017a).

The predominance of Foucault's influence in critical development studies had two important consequences. First, for three decades it eclipsed the work of other important critical thinkers – such as Heidegger, Derrida and Lacan – whose insights could complement and exponentially increase the contribution of post-development. Second, it focused attention on epistemological aspects – on the situated position of the subject and the power dynamics resulting from it – and disregarded ontological questions about the being and nature of both the subject and the object. Only recently have some influential critical development scholars started fathoming the immense potential of an ontological inquiry into development practices, in three parallel lines. The first is the work of Ilan Kapoor drawing on Jacques Lacan and Slavoj Žižek (2013, 2014, 2015a, 2015b, 2017, 2018a, 2018b and 2020). Second, Escobar incorporated Heidegger's philosophy into his Foucauldian critical approach to development (2018 and 2020). Third, Swyngedouw (2014a, 2014b, 2019), Ziai (2004, 2009) and McKinnon (2005, 2006, 2007, 2008) draw on the work of Ernesto Laclau and/or Chantal Mouffe on the topics of radical democracy, the post-political, empty signifiers and so on.

This present work contributes to the third line by going back to the early 1990s with two parallel objectives. First, I seek to reassess Laclau's critical reflection on the West's endless quest for a better world referenced above, and to choose the turn at the crossroads that Foucauldian post-development did *not* – i.e., to follow the path of an *ontological inquiry* into development discourses. My second objective is to critically analyse the birth of the United Nations Development Programme's (UNDP's) human development framework in 1990, and to expose the ontological assumptions made in (and the political function of) the 26 global Human Development Reports (HDRs) it has published so far. In the next section I introduce the UNDP and its discourse on development, and then discuss the key characteristics of the ontological inquiry.

The UNDP and the Human Development Framework

The UNDP was created in 1965 to consolidate and coordinate the UN's emerging development system. For decades, this programme has attracted external funding and administered the UN's technical assistance for development (Murphy, 2006; Stokke, 2009; Browne, 2011). In the early 1990s, it became an influential figure in international development debates. After a decade of growth-centred development planning and structural adjustment strategies led by the Bretton Woods institutions (the International Monetary Fund and the World Bank), in 1990 the UNDP published the first HDR and presented the *human development framework*. This new framework was based on Amartya Sen's capabilities approach (e.g., Sen 1987, 1992), and aimed to relocate people to the centre of development strategies. According to the UNDP, development was not merely an economic issue to be solved by promoting economic growth and structural adjustments. On the contrary, it involves increasing people's freedom to choose and act – that is to say, development entails enhancing people's capabilities and creating opportunities to use them (Fukuda-Parr & Shiva Kumar, 2009). Together with the new development framework, in the 1990 HDR, the UNDP presented a new way to quantify development using the Human Development Index (HDI). Moving beyond previous conceptions of development that focused mainly on economic growth (i.e., GDP per capita), the UNDP created a threefold index that measured health and education in addition to income (UNDP, 1990: 9–16). This multidimensional index soon caught the attention of both policy makers and academics, and continues to have an important influence on development debates (Ponzio & Ghosh, 2016).

Since 1990, the UNDP has published a global HDR every year except four (2007, 2012, 2017 and 2018); it describes these reports on the back cover as 'independent, analytically and empirically grounded discussions of major development issues, trends and policies' (UNDP, 2019). These reports are written and published by the Human Development Report Office (HDRO) in New York. They review the evolution of all countries in terms of human development, and rank them according to their HDI score. Each report focuses on a specific issue related to human development, such as gender, security, economic growth, human rights, democracy, migration, inequality, or climate change. Due to these reports' emphasis on making people both the means *and the end* of development, they soon became referential among researchers, practitioners, institutions and governments that disagreed with the view and the development strategies of the

Washington Consensus adherents. In 1992, the UNDP supplemented the publication of the global reports with the elaboration and publication of national and regional HDRs. These reports review the most important economic, political, social and cultural problems of medium- and low-development countries. These reports are written by local (national and regional) experts and submitted to the HDRO in Manhattan for approval and publication.[1] So far, the UNDP has published almost 800 national and regional HDRs.[2]

I divide the literature about the human development framework of the UNDP into three groups. First, there is a vast literature on the link between the capabilities approach and the human development framework (e.g., Alkire, 2002; Gasper, 2002, 2004; Deneulin & Shahani, 2009; Nussbaum, 2011; Robeyns, 2017; Stewart et al., 2018; Clark et al., 2019). The second strand of the literature features studies that focus on the UNDP's institutional history and explain the birth and evolution of the human development framework (e.g., Klingebiel, 1999; Murphy, 2006; Jolly et al., 2009; Stokke, 2009; Browne, 2011; Murphy & Browne, 2014; Razeq, 2014; Hirai, 2017). Finally, we find a few works that focus on the content of the global HDRs and on their ability to apprehend global issues (e.g., Haq, 1995; Fukuda-Parr & Shiva Kumar, 2009; Ponzio & Ghosh, 2016; Hirai et al., 2019). This literature precisely describes and analyses the human development approach and the way the UNDP understands it: its agency aspect; its relation with the basic needs approach; its potential for policy-making; its measurement and quantifications, and so on. However, I find three important omissions in this literature. First, although the reflection on human development, social change, progress and inequality implies relying on a specific conceptualization of human beings, society and history, no studies have critically analysed the basic philosophical, anthropological, sociological and cultural assumptions in the HDRs. Second, none of these studies questions the essentialist assumptions of the human development approach. They share the UNDP's ontological approach to social issues, hence their critique glosses over the influence and limitations that such a philosophical stand can generate in the UNDP's understanding of development. Third, although some of these works properly locate the birth of the human development framework historically, none of them contributes a critical reading of the key political function that the HDRs played in stabilizing the post-Cold War status quo. The HDRs are always interpreted as a reaction to the structural adjustment strategies by the Washington Consensus adherents, but never as a discursive device intended to solidify the international power structures during the 1990s and 2000s. This book seeks to fill this gap in the literature by exploring the ontological assumptions in the HDRs, the limitations these assumptions generate and the political function of these reports.

To do so, I focus on the 26 global HDRs, which further develop the human development framework each year and advance the insights that then are reproduced in the national and regional reports.[3] These reports have four different parts: the Foreword, written by the UNDP's administrator; the Overview, in which the HDR team summarizes the most important ideas; the 5–7 chapters that form the body of the report; and the statistical annex, where the HDI scores and much other development-related statistical information is presented. Each of these parts contributes different kinds of information to the critical analysis of the UNDP's discourse. The chapters are the most important source of information: they are key to both understanding the structure of the UNDP's discourse and studying its evolution over time. The chapters reflect on how the selected topic for that report (migration, inequality, sustainability, etc.) links to human development; they back up these reflections with empirical, quantitative data; they propose measures and policies to promote human development; and they further advance the human development framework.

The Overview is of the utmost importance for the analysis in this book. This 10–20 page text highlights the most important messages of the report: I generally assumed that if any discursive critical element found in the chapters also appeared in the Overview, this indicated it was not only important for my research, but also for the authors of the report. In this sense, the Overview helped validate my analysis of the chapters.

Although it is usually very short (1 or 2 pages), the Foreword is key to understanding the evolution of the HDRs and assessing their political function. In this section, the UNDP administrator highlights and briefly explains – in a slightly less formal style than the chapters and the Overview – the key insights of the report. It is a kind of 'welcome' to the reader with rich information about how the UNDP understands the past, present and future of global issues, and how the administration locates the UNDP and its commitment within this context.

I examined the content of the statistical annexes the least. This book thoroughly analyses the assumptions behind the design of the HDI and the fact that the UNDP considers itself entitled to score and rank every country in the world. However, I do not analyse the scores themselves or the evolution of the rankings – just the logic behind this statistical classification and distribution.

Ontological essentialism

To introduce the theoretical framework that sustains the critical inquiry in this book, I focus on the second important aspect in the early 1990s: the ontological path in development studies that the Foucauldian post-development approach did not take. Since the 16th and 17th centuries, the Western philosophical tradition has focused strongly on epistemological issues (questions of knowing) at the expense of ontological inquiries (questions of being and existing) (Tarnas, 1991: 282–320). As a consequence, philosophy evolved on the basis of a sharp division between the subject (the one who knows) and the object (the known). This dualism reinforced an essentialist understanding of reality: it was assumed that the object has certain specific essential characteristics that make it what it is: a stone is a stone because it has such and such objective characteristics, a number is a number because it has such and such objective characteristics, and so on. Accordingly, knowing becomes a matter of grasping these essential characteristics – that is to say, an epistemological encounter between the subject and the essential traits of the object. Human beings play a dual role within this framework: on the one hand, they are the subject (the knower); on the other hand, they are one object among many others (a knowable being). Hence, according to mainstream Western philosophical and scientific traditions, *humans are rational beings* – i.e., a thinking body.

This philosophical position has implicit ontological assumptions: it implies that the object is constituted through its essential characteristics. For instance, regardless of any other consideration, a stone is a stone because it has certain essential traits *that make it a stone*. The work of Martin Heidegger challenged these essentialist assumptions and renewed interest in ontology. He challenged the rigid division between subject and object:

> (He) initiated a shift from questions regarding being-qua-*understanding* to questions regarding being-qua-*being*. This shift is feasible only if the disembodied position of an outer-wordly calculating mind, entirely detached from the affairs under analysis, is abandoned. As soon as we start implicating ourselves in the process of interrogation – by asserting the locatedness of our own vantage point – we abandon our research for the conditions of true knowledge and begin interrogating our own conditions.
>
> (Marchart, 2018: 9)

Heidegger problematized the oversimplified Cartesian categories of nature (*res extensa*) and mind (*res cogitans*) that 'obliterate(d) both the specific nature of human beings and that of the objects they encounter' (Mulhall, 2005: 7). The subject was no longer a disembodied reason that seeks pure and objective knowledge, and objects were no longer mere containers of knowable essential and objective traits. Heidegger explained the existence of human beings – the *Dasein* – as beings who have been thrown into a pre-existing world of meanings and practices (Heidegger, 1962: 188–195). From this perspective, the essence of human beings and objects does not comprise a list of positive properties. On the contrary, the essence of humans is their ability to render the world meaningful and to make sense of their own existence (Howarth, 2013: 97), and the object's identity is conferred by the particular systems of meaning within which it is constituted (Glynos and Howarth, 2007: 109). For example, depending on the context, a *person* holding a *stone* in his hands can be a malefactor with a projectile, a worker with a brick, a guy who picked up a valueless object from the ground, or a prestigious artist showing her latest ridiculously expensive sculpture to the public. That is to say, meaning, significance and identity are not objective, but are relative and contingent 'to a particular set of meaningful practices' (Howarth, 2013: 93). For this reason, the work of Heidegger turned the focus of philosophy from questions about truthful knowledge – epistemology: e.g., how can I apprehend the essence of a stone? – to an inquiry of the beings of things and the beings of humans – ontology: e.g., what am I assuming when I say that this is a stone, and from what standpoint am I speaking? In the social sciences, this involved shifting attention from the methodology to an inquiry about the ontological assumptions within the basic concepts mobilized in the investigation:

> From a Heideggerian point of view, then, all theories and approaches in the social and political sciences, including positivist social science approaches, presuppose a distinctive ontology, which structures their more specific theories and explanations.
>
> (Glynos and Howarth, 2007: 109)

That is to say, any epistemological approach to an object implicitly accepts specific ontological assumptions – a concrete conceptualization of reality, and of the being of the things and of the subject. On the contrary, Heidegger's work opened up a new philosophical field in which the former disembodied subject became a being searching for meaning, submerged in a pre-existing set of historically constructed categories and explanations of the world, which she can either uncritically accept or critically problematize.

The importance of meaning and significance in Heidegger's philosophy has been conflated with the work of many other important philosophers of the early 20th century – especially that of the late Ludwig Wittgenstein – in what Richard Rorty called 'the linguistic turn' (Rorty, 1967). This philosophical trend reflected on how language, linguistic constructions and symbolic systems shape the existence of human beings. For example, Jacques Derrida and Ernesto Laclau's post-structuralist work focused on how humans make sense of reality by constructing meaningful representations of the world, and on the ontological assumptions implied in such a construction. Drawing on the work of Ferdinand de Saussure, they developed a relational (not essentialist) understanding of reality, in which the identity and existence of the subject and object are constituted through their relations with other subjects and objects – not on the basis of an alleged inherent essence. Such a theoretical framework relies on the idea that reality is a relational field 'marked by radical contingency, where radical contingency refers to the inherent (as opposed to accidental) instability of an object's identity' (Glynos & Howarth, 2007: 109). I further explain the relational perspective, the sense of Derrida's deconstruction and the political analysis of Laclau in Chapter 1.

There is an ontological dimension in Foucault's work too, especially when he focuses 'on the cultural practices that *made us what we are*' (Dreyfus and Rabinow, 1982: 122, emphasis added). However, post-development researchers did not investigate the ontological dimension of the French philosopher's work, but rather his epistemological critique, in terms of episteme, subject positions, knowledge–power dynamics, bio-power and governmentality. As explained above, only recently have a few influential critical development thinkers proposed analyses of development practices that draw on this contingent and relational ontological basis. I use this theoretical framework to analyse and explain the relationship between the universal and the particular in development discourses, and the West's endless quest to transform the (indomitable) world.

Overall logic and argumentative structure of the book

For the reasons explained above, in this book I conduct a critical analysis of the UNDP's human development framework from the post-structuralist discourse analysis perspective proposed by Derrida and Laclau. More precisely, (1) I assess and deconstruct the symbolic representation of the world that the UNDP constructed over almost three decades in the global HDRs; (2) I expose the ontological assumptions implied in their representation of reality; and (3) I reflect on the political consequences of both the symbolic representation and the ontological assumptions. Hence, the question that animates this book is: *what are the ontological assumptions in the symbolic representation of the world constructed by the UNDP in the HDRs, and what are their political consequences?*

To answer this question, I divide the book into five chapters and a conclusion. Chapter 1 introduces the theoretical and methodological framework of the book's critical inquiry by explaining the key concepts in the work of Derrida and Laclau – i.e., discourse, relationality, contingency, antagonism, transcendental signified, binary oppositions and deconstruction. The chapter exposes the essentialist assumptions of the human development framework and describes the structure of the UNDP's discourse – which is deconstructed in the following chapters.

Chapter 2 looks back to the origins of the UNDP's discourse. It analyses the genealogy of the human development discourse and shows that it reproduces the essentialist assumptions of the late 19th and early 20th centuries' evolutionist sociology – i.e., Herbert Spencer and Talcott Parsons' understanding of human beings, social change and history. The chapter draws on Clifford Geertz's critique of their work to show that the structure of (and the logics within) the UNDP's discourse limit its ability to apprehend the complexity of current societies. The UNDP tackles the 21st century global society using the sociological assumptions of the colonial, Victorian 19th century.

Chapter 3 focuses on the present – more precisely, on the UNDP's conceptualization of the individual and its role in activating what it calls 'the virtuous circle' of human development. The analysis shows that the HDRs recount, year after year, that inequality is growing both within and between countries. However, the UNDP continues to insist that increasing productivity – rather than promoting fairer distribution – should solve the problem. The chapter shows that the UNDP's discourse is exhausted and cannot properly apprehend actual global problems.

Chapter 4 analyses how the UNDP envisions the future by focusing on how the term 'culture' is articulated in the human development framework. The inquiry shows that the UNDP echoes Fukuyama's theses on the end of history, and that the HDRs construct a symbolic identity division between the liberal West and the rest of the world. Such a representation of the world presents the West as the expression of the universal future and the rest as examples of past particularisms.

Hence, one of the main contradictions of the human development reports is that the UNDP explicitly defends the notion that diversity is positive for human development; however, it implicitly assumes that the West – more specifically, its allegedly ideal and universal cultural values and principles – is the example that should guide the evolution of humankind.

Chapter 5 shows that the three temporal perspectives discussed in Chapters 2, 3 and 4 – past, present and future, respectively – merge to implement the political function of the HDRs: the construction of a symbolic representation of the world to stabilize the status quo during the transition from the bipolar Cold War to the unipolar post-Cold War period. The inquiry in this chapter explains that the UNDP strengthened and consolidated the development–underdevelopment antagonistic division of the world that replaced the liberalism–communism antagonism of the bipolar period. Finally, the conclusion contributes a few notes about how to construct a relational perspective on global issues.

Notes

1 For a detailed analysis of the elaboration of the national and regional reports, and a critical review of the participatory research methodology the UNDP used in their development and publication, see Telleria 2020.
2 All the global, national, and regional HDRs are freely available on the website of the HDRO: www.hdr.undp.org/
3 Personal communication: William Orme, HDRO Chief of Communications and Publishing, April 2013, New York.

References

Alkire, S. (2002) *Valuing Freedoms: Sen's Capability Approach and Poverty Reduction*, Oxford: Oxford University Press.

Browne, S. (2011) *The UN Development Programme and System*, Abingdon: Routledge.

Clark, D.A., M. Biggeri & A.A. Frediani (eds) (2019) *The Capability Approach, Empowerment and Participation: Concepts, Methods and Applications*, London: Palgrave Macmillan.

Deneulin, S. & L. Shahani (eds) (2009) *An Introduction to the Human Development and Capability Approach: Freedom and Agency*, London: Earthscan.

Dreyfus, H. & P. Rabinow (1982) *Michel Foucault: Beyond Structuralism and Hermeneutics*, Toronto: Harvester Wheatsheaf.

Escobar, A. (1995) *Encountering Development. The Making and Unmaking of the Third World*, Princeton (NJ): Princeton University Press.

Escobar, A. (2018) *Designs for the Pluriverse. Radical Interdependence, Autonomy, and the Making of Worlds*, Durham (NC): Duke University Press.

Escobar, A. (2020) *Pluriversal Politics. The Real and the Possible*, Durham (NC): Duke University Press.

Fukuda-Parr, S. & A.K. Shiva Kumar (2009) *Handbook of Human Development*, New Delhi: Oxford University Press.

Gasper, D. (2002) Is Sen's capability approach an adequate basis for considering human development? *Review of Political Economy*, 14 (4), 435–461.

Gasper, D. (2004) *The Ethics of Development*. Edinburgh: Edinburgh University Press.

Glynos, J. & D. Howarth (2007) *Logics of Critical Explanation in Social and Political Theory*, Abingdon: Routledge.

Haq, M.U. (1995) *Reflections on Human Development*, Oxford: Oxford University Press.

Heidegger, M. (1962) *Being and Time*, Oxford: Basil Blackwell.

Hirai, T. (2017) *The Creation of the Human Development Approach*, Cham (Switzerland): Palgrave Macmillan.

Hirai, T., F. Comim & R. Jolly (2019) Rescuing human development from a lip-service syndrome, *Development Policy Review*, doi:10.1111/dpr.12478

Howarth, D. (2013) *Poststructuralism and after: Structure, Subjectivity and Power*, Basingstoke: Palgrave Macmillan.

Jolly, R., L. Emmerij & T.G. Weiss (2009) *UN Ideas That Changed the World*, Bloomington (IN): Indiana University Press.

Kapoor, I. (2013) *Celebrity Humanitarianism: The Ideology of Global Charity*, New York: Routledge.

Kapoor, I. (2014) Psychoanalysis and development: contributions, examples, limits, *Third World Quarterly*, 35 (7), 1120–1143.

Kapoor, I. (2015a) The queer Third World, *Third World Quarterly*, 36 (9), 1611–1628.

Kapoor, I. (2015b) What 'drives' capitalist development? *Human Geography*, 8 (3), 66–78.

Kapoor, I. (2017) Cold critique, faint passion, bleak future: post-development's surrender to global capitalism, *Third World Quarterly*, 38 (12), 2664–2683.

Kapoor, I. (ed.) (2018a) *Psychoanalysis and the Global*, Lincoln (NE): University of Nebraska Press.

Kapoor, I. (2018b) Žižek, antagonism and politics now: three recent controversies, *International Journal of Žižek Studies*, 12 (1) (online).

Kapoor, I. (2020) *Confronting Desire: Psychoanalysis and International Development*, Ithaca (NY): Cornell University Press.

Klingebiel, S. (1999) *Effectiveness and Reform of the United Nations Development Programme*, London: Frank Cass.

Kothari, A., A. Salleh, A. Escobar, F. Demaria & A. Acosta (2019) *Pluriverse: A Post-development Dictionary*, New Delhi: Tulika Books.

Laclau, E. (1996) *Emancipation(s)*, London: Verso.

Marchart, O. (2018) *Thinking Antagonism: Political Ontology after Laclau*, Edinburgh: Edinburgh University Press.

McKinnon, K. (2005) (Im)mobilization and hegemony: 'hill tribe' subjects and the 'Thai' state, *Social and Cultural Geography*, 6 (1), 31–46.

McKinnon, K. (2006) An orthodoxy of 'the local': post-colonialism, participation and professionalism in northern Thailand, *The Geographical Journal*, 172 (1), 22–34.

McKinnon, K. (2007) Postdevelopment, professionalism, and the politics of participation, *Annals of the Association of American Geographers*, 97 (4), 772–785.

McKinnon, K. (2008) Taking post-development theory to the field: issues in development research, northern Thailand, *Asia Pacific Viewpoint*, 49 (3), 281–293.

Mulhall, S. (2005) *Heidegger and Being and Time*, New York: Routledge.

Mulhall, S. (2013) *Heidegger's Being and Time*, Abingdon: Routledge.

Murphy, C. (2006) *The United Nations Development Programme: A Better Way?*Cambridge: Cambridge University Press.

Murphy, C. & S. Browne (2014) *UNDP: Reviving a Practical Human Development Organization*, Governance and Sustainable Issue Brief Series, 9, Boston: Center for Governance and Sustanablity, University of Massachussetts.

Nussbaum, M. (2011) *Creating Capabilities: The Human Development Approach*, Cambridge (MA): Belknap.

Ponzio, R. & A. Ghosh (2016) *Human Development and Global Institutions. Evolution, Impact, Reform*, Abingdon: Routledge.

Razeq, Z.M. (2014) *UNDP's Engagement with the Private Sector, 1994–2011*, New York: Palgrave Macmillan.

Rist, G. (1996) *The History of Development: From Western Origins to Global Faith*, London: Zed Books.

Robeyns, I. (2017) *Wellbeing, Freedom and Social Justice: The Capability Approach Re-Examined*, Cambridge: Open Book.

Rorty, R. (ed.) (1967) *The Linguistic Turn: Recent Essays in Philosophical Method*, Chicago: University of Chicago Press.

Sachs, W. (ed.) (1992) *The Development Dictionary: A Guide to Knowledge as Power*, New York: Zed Books.

Sen, A. (1987) *Commodities and Capabilities*, New Delhi: Oxford University Press.

Sen, A. (1992) *Inequality Reexamined*, Oxford: Clarendon Press.

Stewart, F., G. Ranis & E. Samman (2018) *Advancing Human Development: Theory and Practice*, Oxford: Oxford University Press.

Stokke, O. (2009) *The UN and Development. From Aid to Cooperation*, Bloomington (IN): Indiana University Press.

Swyngedouw, E. (2014a) De-politicization ('the political'), in G. D'Alisa, F. Demaria & G. Kallis (eds), *Degrowth: A Vocabulary for a New Era*, London: Routledge, pp. 90–93.

Swyngedouw, E. (2014b) Where is the political? Insurgent mobilisations and the incipient 'return of the political', *Space and Polity*, 18 (2), 122–136.

Swyngedouw, E. (2019) The perverse lure of autocratic postdemocracy, *South Atlantic Quarterly*, 18 (2), 267–286.

Tarnas, R. (1991) *The Passion of the Western Mind: Understanding the Ideas That Have Shaped Our World View*, New York: Harmony Books.

Telleria, J. (2020) Development and participation: whose participation? A critical analysis of the UNDP's participatory research methods, *European Journal of Development Research*, published online 29 May 2020.

UN (1945) *Charter of the United Nations*, San Francisco: United Nations.

UN (2015) *2030 Agenda for Sustainable Development*, New York: United Nations.

UNDP (1990) *Human Development Report. Concept and Measuring of Human Development*, New York: Oxford University Press.

UNDP (2019) *Human Development Report. Beyond Income, Beyond Averages, Beyond Today: Inequalities in Human Development in the 21st Century*, New York: UNDP.

Ziai, A. (2004) The ambivalence of post-development: between reactionary populism and radical democracy, *Third World Quarterly*, 25 (6), 1045–1060.

Ziai, A. (2009) 'Development': projects, power, and a poststructuralist perspective, *Alternatives*, 34, 183–201.

Ziai, A. (2017a) 'I am not a post-developmentalist, but …' the influence of post-development on development studies, *Third World Quarterly*, 38 (12), 2719–2734.

Ziai, A. (2017b) Post-development 25 years after *The Development Dictionary*, *Third World Quarterly*, 38 (12), 2547–2558.

1 (The absence of) development

> Democracy and human development (...) are both more a journey than
> a destination – a promise rather than a list.
>
> (*Human Development Report 2002*)

In *Contingency, Hegemony, Universality: Contemporary Dialogues on
the Left* (2000), Ernesto Laclau explains that the intellectual history of
the 20th century began with three 'illusions of immediacy' – analytic
philosophy, phenomenology and structuralism – which assumed it was
possible to immediately access the 'things themselves' (Laclau, 2000:
74). According to this essentialist perspective, the subject (the knower)
can have non-mediated access to the object (the known), which is the
starting point for the production of true, objective and veritable
knowledge. Laclau traces the evolution of these three philosophical
traditions and concludes that 'at some stage, in all three, the illusion of
immediacy disintegrates and gives way to one or other form of thought
in which *discursive mediation becomes primary and constitutive*'
(Laclau, 2000: 74, emphasis added). As explained in the Introduction,
Heidegger's existential phenomenology moved the ontological focus
from the object to the situated nature of the subject (the Dasein) and
its existence in a context of historically meaningful practices. In parallel, the post-analytical work of the late Wittgenstein and post-structuralist inquiries by Derrida and Foucault, among others, showed that
language was not a direct and transparent representation of reality –
where words simply name things and their essence – but a constructed
structure of signification that mediates between the subject and the
object. These critical ontological and linguistic insights eroded the
conviction of 'the existence of a presence or reality that is simply given
to consciousness' and shifted the attention of Western philosophy and
social sciences to 'the constructed, mediated and ultimately contingent
character of all objectivity' (Howarth, 2015: 3).

Since this linguistic turn during the second half of the 20th century, and the consolidation of 'discourse' as a central category in philosophy and social sciences in the 1970s, there has been considerable debate about this category and, accordingly, about the nature and status of discourse analysis. In this book, I follow the comprehensive understanding of discourse proposed by post-structuralist thinkers such as Jacques Derrida and Ernesto Laclau, who maintain that discourse is *a constructed relational and contingent symbolic system that mediates between individuals and reality*. Accordingly, discourse analysis involves examining the historical and political construction and functioning of such a symbolic order.

Four key concepts deserve special attention in this approach to discourse analysis: *relationality, mediation, contingency* and *practice*. In order to explain the importance of these concepts, this chapter reviews the work of Derrida and Laclau. First, I describe Ferdinand de Saussure's understanding of language as a basis for explaining Derrida's approach to discourse and deconstruction. Then, I introduce Laclau's perspective on the political nature of discourse and the discursive constitution of political identities. Finally, I present the discursive structure of the global reports of the United Nations Development Programme (UNDP), which I deconstruct in Chapters 2 to 5.

Saussure: language, mediation and relationality

To explain Derrida's conceptualization of language and discourse, I start with a two-step introduction to Saussure's work. First, let us recall one of those moments when a word is repeated so many times that it seems meaningless. The word – 'book' for example – becomes a mere sound (a signifier) with *no necessary relationship* to the object it refers to (the signified). Books could be called 'blups' or 'merks' (different signifiers) as long as every speaker accepts that they refer to the same signified concept. One of Saussure's most important structuralist linguistic findings was that the relationship between the signifier and the signified is arbitrary; this idea strongly influenced Derrida's work (Howarth, 2013: 25).

Second, although a person may not know the meaning of *liburu*, if they are told it means 'book' in Basque, they will understand. Why? Because now they can link this signifier to those with known meanings – such as book, paper, words, letter, ink, cover, text, translation, and Basque. They will conclude that *liburu* is an object with a cover, white sheets, black ink letters, and words forming a text, which in English is translated as 'book'. This is another of Saussure's important insights: he described language as 'a system of interdependent terms in which the value of each term results solely from the simultaneous presence of the others' (Saussure, 1974: 114). This is the first of the four key concepts highlighted above: language is *a relational web of meanings* that is generally accepted by its speakers. For that reason, making a signifier meaningful involves properly relating it to other signifiers. The entry in a dictionary for a given word does not give us the thing it refers to: the entry for 'book' does not put the idea of a book directly in my mind. It instead links the word 'book' to other words in a way that constructs an idea of what a book is. For example, while most people may not know what the word 'peplomer' means, adding the description that it is the spike in the capsule of a virus that binds it to the host helps them understand; they do not need to see a peplomer to know what it means. The web of meanings of known words – spike, virus, capsule, bind, host – thus defines the meaning of the new term. To understand what peplomer means, I simply need to locate it within an existing web of meaningful terms. In this sense, a term's signifying ability does not directly derive from the object or idea it refers to, but from its relationship with other meaningful terms.

Does this mean that we do not need to have contact with reality (with a real book or a real peplomer, in this case) to determine the meaning of a signifier? Does Saussure mean that we live in a kind of semiotic cloud with no contact with reality? No. His understanding of language is not a nihilist idealism that is detached from material reality and common sense (Howarth, 2013: 93). He instead maintains that our contact with reality *is necessarily mediated* by a web of meaningful terms called discourse – the second key concept. Every object, and every action we perceive and understand, is meaningful to us only if we articulate it in an existing symbolic system. The fact that discourse mediates between individuals and reality does not imply that I can properly relate to reality on the basis of *any* discourse. Discourses are not random inventions that are detached from reality: real objects and actions (books, peplomers, etc.) exist, and their existence directly influences the meaning of these terms and their articulation in the symbolic system. An individual would not be able to understand what a peplomer is – and how viruses bind to the host, why we get ill, how vaccines work and so on – by linking it to concepts such as cake, fiord, poetry or car engine. A discourse is only effective (properly mediates) inasmuch as it constructs a web of meanings that offers a coherent explanation of (and enables a satisfactory relationship with) reality.

Derrida: contingency and *différance*

So far, Saussure and Derrida's approaches to language generally concur. However, an important aspect turned Saussure's structuralism into Derrida's *post*-structuralism. I use the example of the evolution of telephone technology to illustrate this shift. The signifier 'phone' could refer to either a landline device with a cable and rotary dial or a smartphone with internet access. Users could describe them in different ways, and would likely explain that the smartphone is an evolution of the rotary phone. The conclusion would likely be 'they are the same and different at the same time!'

Derrida's understanding of meaning plays with this notion of *being the same and different at the same time* (Derrida, 1981: 33; Glendinning, 2011: 62). Saussure's focus was on language *as a product*, whereas Derrida understands it *as a process of production* (Howarth, 2013: 39–40). Derrida explains that the relational character of a discourse is not only synchronic; it is also diachronic. The meaning of 'phone' not only depends on the meaning of many other terms (synchronic), but also on its previous meanings and on the possibility of having different ones in the future (diachronic). For Derrida, every term in a discourse is always open to otherness (Staten, 1984: 18). Paradoxically, the possibility that a term becomes something that it is not, is part of its inherent nature (Staten, 1984: 17). This is because a web of meanings is constantly being rearticulated. Once a new term is inserted into the existing web, the web itself and its elements change. That is to say, the articulation of a new concept forces a re-articulation of the whole web of meanings. Thus, a term's meaning is contingent on the changing meanings of the other terms in the discursive structure. This is the third key concept: meaning belongs to the *contingent* realm of becoming, where fixity is the exception.

An example is the word 'atom'. The definition of this term – its articulation in a meaningful web – changed when the electron was discovered. Ancient Greeks defined atom by linking it to matter, division and limit; modern scientists relate it to energy, protons, orbit and speed. That is to say, the insertion of the term electron changed the meaning of the term atom, and, consequently, the whole web of meanings. In this sense, Derrida would say that when Democritus wrote 'atom' about 24 centuries ago, *the term was open to mean something else*; indeed, that is the contingent nature of the meaning of any term. When I read Democritus' work now, the word atom brings an image to my mind (the signified) that is different to the one Democritus had in mind. The same applies to the example of the phone discussed above: the meaning of the signifier 'phone' not only refers to other signifiers synchronically – call, numbers, internet, and so on. It also refers to the same signifier in the past (which is no longer) and in the future (the possibility of having a different meaning, which is not yet). The word 'phone' (or any other word) is constantly open to recontextualization and rearticulation. That is the sense of radical contingency: the meaning of each term depends on the meaning of other terms, which are in turn based on their relations with other terms in the structure. That is why discourse is unavoidably marked by instability and constant rearticulation.

In this way, Derrida advanced Saussure's insights and proposed a new way to understand language, meaning and discourses, confronted with the traditional essentialist and nominalist perspective previous to Saussure (Howarth, 2000: 31). The latter assumes that objects have an essence, that reality has an inherent and stable order, and that language can reproduce it in our mind. Within the essentialist logic, words precisely reproduce real objects: they simply relate names to things, concepts, actions, and so on. Accordingly, they assume that the structure of language parallels the structure of reality (Derrida, 1982: 183; Staten, 1984: 7), and that, in an ideal, optimal epistemological encounter with reality, we would be able to precisely reproduce it in our mind. According to the essentialist perspective, language would enable direct, objective and fully transparent contact with reality. On the contrary, Derrida explains that language is an interface that systematically mediates between individuals and reality. Accordingly, *our understanding of reality systematically reproduces the structure of language* – which might, or might not, be the same as the structure of reality. Since language is a complex and contingent relational structure that is systematically opened to otherness – to change, to rearticulation, to recontextualization – our understanding of reality will inevitably be contingent on and open to constant rearticulation. This does not mean that language is an arbitrary structure and that, accordingly, Derrida is arguing that any proposition is as valid as any other. His understanding of language does not summon the arrival of discursive anarchy. If that were the case, communication and coexistence would be impossible, and after reading a paragraph you would have thrown this book into the bin (if you have got this far, it means you did not). Derrida is instead making the case that any attempt to produce a single, fixed, stable and transparent representation of reality is necessarily condemned to fail.

Critically analysing the structure of language and meaning takes us from an epistemological realm characterized by a single, fixed approach to an essential reality (e.g., positivism) to one that features the coexistence of diverse (not infinite) and contingent (not arbitrary) approaches to reality. Derrida coined the term *différance* to explain the contingent, complex and relational nature of language and our understanding of reality. It mixes the French words for difference (*différence* in French) and deferred (*différée* in French). *Différance* as 'difference' stresses the synchronic relational character of language: the meaning of every term is constantly open to other terms because its current meaning is constituted by its relationship to them. *Différance* as 'to defer' stresses the diachronic nature of language: the meaning of every term (atom, phone) is constantly open to something that is no longer (Democritus' atom, an old phone) and to something that is not yet (future rearticulations) (Howarth, 2013: 53).

The search for stability: binary oppositions and the transcendental signified

If, according to Derrida, our understanding of the world is necessarily contingent and unstable, how did traditional essentialist approaches to reality explain the world? How did they avoid contingency and instability? In general, Derrida's philosophical work exposes how the Western epistemological essentialist tradition – which aimed to find a way to purely, transparently and truthfully represent reality – is inexorably affected by the contingent and unstable nature of language, and, accordingly, the logic of *différance*. According to Derrida, the essentialist approach sought stability in two complementary ways: by constructing binary oppositions that are assumed to represent reality, and by relying on a transcendental signified that stabilizes, sustains and governs the structure of meanings. I now explain these important concepts.

Derrida critically analyses key Western philosophical and scientific works and exposes the key importance of specific binary oppositions within them. These works systematically tackle reality by constructing oppositions such as rational/irrational, true/false, soul/body, light/darkness, new/old, day/night, tall/short, strong/weak, and masculine/feminine. Derrida explains that, contrary to the essentialist perspective, these binary oppositions do not offer a direct representation of reality. On the contrary, they fall into the logic of *différance*. Each of the terms in the binary opposition, Derrida explains, is relationally defined and necessarily open to otherness. That is to say, each of the elements in the opposition systematically *needs* and *negates* the other term. For example, it is impossible to think of rationality without explicitly or implicitly appealing to irrationality; however, irrationality negates rationality, and vice versa. In other words, each term is necessarily and relationally open to its negation: the term rational would not exist in a meaningful way without the existence of its opposite – irrational. Thus, these binary oppositions are not natural and transparent representations of reality, but categories that are relationally constructed and open to otherness and contingency.

There is yet another problem that hinders the essentialist epistemological project. Derrida explains that every binary opposition is hierarchically structured: one of the terms is privileged over the other – rationality is privileged over irrationality, true over false, strong over weak, and so on. This hierarchical distribution does not happen arbitrarily: on the contrary, Derrida explains that it is based on the assumption that a specific value is more (but not fully) *present* in the privileged term and, accordingly, more (but not totally) *absent* in the other (Derrida, 1981: 26). For example, rationality is privileged over irrationality because, for instance, coherence is more present in (but not synonymous with) rationality and more absent in (but not an antonym of) irrationality. The necessary reference to another concept to sustain the implicit hierarchy of each binary opposition generates an anti-essentialist conundrum. One binary opposition (rational/irrational) refers to another binary opposition (coherence/incoherence), which in turn refers to another; the list could go on *ad infinitum*. The need for a present/absent value that structures each binary opposition implies an endless deferral that exposes the inherent contingent nature of discourses, which, by definition, essentialist approaches cannot accept. Derrida explains that in order to solve this dangerous conundrum, essentialist perspectives use a wildcard called 'transcendental signified' (Derrida, 1978: 280; 1981: 29; 2016: 53).

Archimedes said that if we had a firm spot on which to stand, we would be able to move the earth. Obviously, this spot should be *outside* the earth – external to the body to move. According to Derrida, this is what essentialist discourses do to stabilize the otherwise contingent and unstable nature of any discursive structure: they posit an external spot that sustains the entire discursive structure (Derrida, 1978: 351–355; Bradley, 2008: 31). The transcendental signified is a signified (an idea, a concept) beyond questioning – with absolute discursive authority – that acts as the stable and solid foundation of the discourse. It is not part of the discursive structure; rather, it is the primary truth that governs the entire structure from outside. It sustains the hierarchy of the binary oppositions and sets the purpose of the entire discourse. It is the self-sufficient signified of all signifiers (Spivak, in Derrida, 2016:

lxxxv). For example, the dogmatic assumption that a transcendental being called God exists is the transcendental signified of religious discourses: it sustains and governs the entire discourse; however, the discourse assumes (but does not demonstrate) it.

The fact that the transcendental signified governs the entire discourse but does not belong to it generates a discursive paradox: the transcendental signified is necessary... but *ultimately lacking*. It is present in the sense that it makes the discourse cogent, but ultimately lacking because it points far into an ideal horizon that can never be attained – e.g., the Kingdom of God. The transcendental signified is an ideal horizon in which each term, each binary opposition, and the entire structure attain perfect coherence and solidity; it is the end towards which every meaning is constantly deferred; it is the promise of the full presence of truth, of pure and unmediated contact with reality, and of clear-cut and transparent representation. However, as a horizon it is unreachable in practice: it defines the purpose and governs the entire discursive structure, but is always absent. It is an unattainable and perpetual 'yet to come'.

Overall, Derrida concludes that essentialist discourses avoid contingency and instability by posing an unreachable discursive element that is assumed, but not demonstrated. For that reason, his understanding of discourse offers an adequate theoretical framework to explain how meaning is relationally constructed and how essentialist approaches seek to avert the contingent nature of reality by constructing binary oppositions and positing a transcendental signified. As I explain below, Derrida's deconstruction just reveals the trick.

Laclau: the constitution of political identities

In the definition of discourse outlined at the beginning of the chapter, I emphasized that it is a *constructed* symbolic system – the fourth key concept. As explained above, for Derrida, discourse is not a rigid and fixed representation of reality, but an ever-evolving structure that makes reality meaningful. Drawing on the work of Husserl and Heidegger, both Derrida and Laclau explain that the subject can either accept the inherited sedimented[1] categories that are portrayed as natural and self-evident, or challenge them by constructing alternative discourses that make reality meaningful in an different way (Derrida, 1978: 32; Laclau, 1996: 87). The fact that discourses are constructed – i.e., the fact that they are a practice – opens up the possibility of articulating alternative meaningful structures that enable different perspectives on reality (Howarth, 2013: 97). Moreover, the possibility of constructing alternative discourses does not affect only how we understand reality, but how we understand ourselves, and our relationship with reality. Laclau brings the political dimension of the construction and articulation of discourses to the fore by explaining the constitution of political identities – i.e., how individuals understand their existence and their relations with the context; how groups with common principles, perspectives, interests, claims, motivations and objectives constitute themselves as political agents; and how different groups create coalitions to implement their political project.

Laclau parallels the relational constitution of the meaning of a term and the constitution of a political identity. As explained above, for Derrida, each binary opposition is constructed in an antagonistic way: each of the terms in the opposition *needs* and *negates* the other – as is the case for rationality and irrationality, for example. Laclau explains that political identities follow the same logic. The constitution of any political identity – individual or collective – relies on creating an antagonistic relationship. To be constituted, any political identity *needs* an opposite, which, at the same time, *negates* its full constitution. For instance, all political identities rely on an antagonistic relationship that creates a boundary between 'us' and 'them'. Progressives contrast their identity with that of conservatives, as do leftists against right-wing positions, Catholics against Protestants, socialists against capitalists, globalists against localists and so on. This antagonistic relationship implies that each side's political project is systematically threatened by the existence of the other side. In other words, the antagonistic boundary is based on a (not necessarily violent) *conflict* of principles, interests, motivations, claims and objectives. These groups struggle to implement their political project knowing (or assuming) that the success of the opposite group implies the failure of their project. This antagonistic tension animates political identities and struggles, for if both sides come together and reach an agreement, the terms that signify each side tend to disappear. For example, in a society in which everyone agrees that animal rights must be respected, the identity 'animalist' would disappear – or would connote something different – and new identities would emerge based on other tensions and conflicts.

On the basis of this theoretical framework, Laclau explained politics as a process of creating identities and building coalitions (Laclau, 2005: 67–128). In this context, coalition does not exclusively mean political party; Laclau would also consider demonstrators, a group of neighbours against the construction of a road, or the reactionary bourgeoisie to be political coalitions. For him, a successful political project relies on the condensation of multiple groups – which have different and plural claims and demands – into a more encompassing unity. To do so, the project must find and highlight the common thread between the groups – the claims, demands, principles, motivations or interests that, at least precariously, enable a coalition. This process features two important aspects that are key to understanding the critical approach to the UNDP's discourse in this book. The political project (coalition) must:

1   Define a common 'other' with which to create an antagonistic relationship in order to consolidate the precarious coalition (Laclau & Mouffe, 1985: 108–131).
2   Defuse and hide the new coalition's internal antagonisms and tensions by stressing the similarities and common aspects of its members (their equivalences) and overlooking their differences.

To do so, the new project must identify what Laclau calls *an empty signifier* – a term that is specific enough to refer to the entire political project and unite the new group (i.e., to signify the opposition to the menacing 'other') but ambiguous and empty enough to gloss over the group's internal tensions and contradictions (Laclau, 1996: 39). Justice, order, freedom, democracy and truth are examples of possible empty signifiers. On the one hand, they create a clear boundary – for example against those who do not promote justice, those who create disorder, and so on. On the other hand, they are empty enough to enable multiple groups – with different principles, interests and objectives – to accept it as the guiding value that structures the political endeavour of the coalition. Coalition leaders will have to keep it empty, because concrete and specific descriptions of how to achieve justice, how to create order or how to define democracy could trigger differences within the coalition. Development has the proper characteristics of an empty signifier: it is the opposite of underdevelopment – which is generally accepted as negative and dangerous – and, at the same time, it is empty enough to gather different groups under this banner. I argue in this book that this is also the case for the term 'human development'.

It is important not to mix up the transcendental signified and the empty signifier. According to Derrida, the transcendental *signified* is a *concept* (idea) that represents the unreachable ideal horizon – an absolute fullness. It sustains the discursive structure from outside and makes it appear stable and cogent. According to Laclau, an empty *signifier* is the *term* that unites a group of people in their approach to pursuing such an ideal horizon. It is empty and does not represent absolute fullness; it just points far into the ideal horizon. The former is related to the structure of the discourse and defines the end, whereas the latter is a rhetorical tool that unites a group of people under a single banner (Laclau, 2014: 44).

Overall, Laclau's approach to social and political issues has important ontological and practical consequences that contradict the basic assumptions of traditional essentialist perspectives. As explained above, for the latter, social beings (individuals or groups) have certain essential traits that constitute them as such – such as rationality, a soul, free will, basic needs or fundamental rights. On the basis of these essential, universal and common characteristics, it is assumed that a consensus that benefits everyone, at least at a basic (essential) level, is possible. Such a consensus would result in the creation of specific rules and institutions that would respect and nurture the alleged natural essence of human beings – Hobbes, Locke, Rousseau or Rawls' theorization of the social contract are good examples of this political ontology. According to this perspective, development is, in general terms, the advancement towards a society in which the essence of each social being is respected and realized to its maximum potential. In this sense, development would entail both (1) the process of unfolding such an essence and (2) the stage at which the potential of the essence reaches a pre-defined threshold. Laclau's antagonistic and relational approach to social and political issues introduces a different perspective. He does not maintain that human beings are basically different – it is undeniable that we all have common traits, including a body, rational abilities, emotions, skills and needs – but *that we understand ourselves (identity) and our relationships with social and natural reality (political projects) in multiple and diverse legitimate ways.* Thus according to Laclau, we construct a symbolic representation of reality in multiple, diverse ways. Since antagonism and conflict are central aspects in the construction of discourses, they are the constitutive and ineradicable elements of social life – not an alleged universal and common essence. The corollary of Laclau's relational approach is that society is plural and, accordingly, that any political and social order is the result of specific political decisions that benefit some groups at the expense of others – not an essential consensus that benefits all.

Deconstruction and the analysis of Human Development Reports

According to Derrida and Laclau, discourse is a practice: the construction of a symbolic system that mediates between each individual and reality. Moreover, it is a practice that strongly influences other practices: our decisions and actions will change depending on how we understand reality and our relation to it. As mentioned above, political agents either choose to accept the discourse that their culture and historical context presents as natural and self-evident, or to problematize, rethink and rearticulate it. This is the sense of Derrida's deconstruction. Deconstruction problematizes essentialist discourses that are assumed to be natural and self-evident, and demonstrates that they construct binary oppositions based on the implicit assumption of a transcendental signified. Deconstruction shows that once the transcendental signified is detected and called into question, the cracks, clefts, tensions and contradictions of the (allegedly true and solid) essentialist discursive structure emerge. Finally, deconstruction explains that once these contradictions and tensions are critically analysed, the hierarchy of the binary oppositions and the entire discursive structure fall apart, and many (though not infinite) alternative discourses emerge to legitimately explain reality. Deconstruction is not Derrida's struggle for truth: it is instead his critical reading and dismantling of *the discourses on truth*, and the erection of an alternative understanding of reality (Staten, 1984: 26). Laclau explains that 'the role of deconstruction is (…) to *reactivate* the moment of decision that underlies any *sedimented* set of social relations' (Laclau, 1996: 78). Behind any common-sense statement, we find decisions taken under specific conditions – following concrete principles and assumptions – that shaped and consolidated certain discourses at the expense of others. These moments of decision tend to fade away (sediment), making the discourse look natural and a description of 'the way things really are' (Mouffe, 2000: 5). Reactivation is the critical process that brings these decisions to the fore and 'produce(s) a widening of horizons, in so far as other articulations – equally contingent – will also show their possibility' (Laclau, 1996: 87). In this book I draw on the concepts from Derrida and Laclau explained above to reactivate some of the sedimented decisions that laid the essentialist foundation of the UNDP's discourse and deconstruct the human development framework, as presented in the 26 global Human Development Reports (HDRs) published between 1990 and 2019.

In practice, deconstruction does not work by applying external forces to the discursive structure to destroy it. Nor is it a matter of superimposing a new structure – a new truth – over the ruins of the old discourse. Instead, it is a meticulous art that requires patience, attention and very careful reading. It involves generating a precise description of the structure and getting inside it to find both the strongest parts that keep it rigid and the weak elements that warn of an imminent collapse. If properly selected, a small vibration at a very specific point may cause the entire structure to fall apart. Ideally, at the end of this process the parts of the old structure are unbroken and ready to construct in a new way (Spivak, in Derrida, 2016: c).

Accordingly, in my critical analysis I do not contrast 'the truth' of the UNDP with another external truth that I find more veritable. I do not look for statistical data that contradicts the HDRs, or cite alternative sources which demonstrate that the UNDP's descriptions of the situation in certain countries was mistaken. Such a strategy would condemn the book to failure. The UNDP technicians and the staff writing the HDRs have much better information than I do, and much more experience and expertise in working with that information. Therefore I take the critical approach to a different dimension. In the process of interpreting and elaborating its information, the UNDP accepts and reproduces a specific understanding of reality – i.e., a specific discourse. In some cases, specific elements of the reproduced discourse are explicitly explained and championed, such as the capabilities approach. However, in other cases, the UNDP unknowingly accepts and reproduces elements that strongly condition its understanding of reality – for example, the 19th century stratigraphic conceptualization of human beings, as I explain in Chapter 2.

For that reason, I do not create a direct confrontation between my understanding of the world and that of the UNDP; I instead set up *an internal confrontation within the discourse of the UNDP*. I merely provide the boxing ring and a few rules for the fight, and the UNDP becomes its own harshest critic. The analysis in this book is less like a medical procedure and more akin to psychoanalytic therapy: I ask the questions and the UNDP struggles with its own contradictions. Throughout the book I rely on two kinds of bibliographic resources: (1) the philosophers and social scientists who provide me with the tools and the resources to build the boxing ring – or the divan – and (2) the global HDRs published by the UNDP between 1990 and 2019. In Chapters 2 to 5 I extensively use quotes extracted from these reports. As much as possible I allow the UNDP to express itself, which helps ensure my analysis remains loyal to the spirit of deconstruction.

These reports were my only contact with the UNDP for the research in this book. I conducted no interviews and did not contact the staff of the UNDP on purpose. This is a key methodological aspect of deconstruction. My interest is in the *discourse* contained in the HDRs, not what the authors think about development or the reports – or even how these opinions influence and condition their content. It is the reports, not the opinions of their authors, that reproduces a specific understanding of reality, which in turn influences many other practices and how lot of people understand development. Derrida explicitly questions whether there is a coincidence between the intention of the writer – which is supposedly fully present in the text – and the reading and interpretation of the reader (Powell, 2006: 128). That would imply a transparent immediacy that contradicts Derrida and Laclau's understanding of language. On the contrary, deconstruction relies on the certainty that once the text is written, it is open to interpretation – open to otherness – and that this is the natural existence of a text. I focus on the reports because I aim to deconstruct the human development framework of the UNDP as presented in them, not the intention of the writers or the interpretation of the readers, which would have required a very different research approach.

Essentialism and the UNDP's transcendental signified

Before deconstructing the UNDP's discourse in Chapters 2 to 5, the final section of this chapter presents the essentialist foundations of the human development framework, exposes the transcendental signified that sustains the discourse, and introduces the binary opposition and discursive structure to be deconstructed.

As pointed out above, the UNDP constructs the human development discourse from an essentialist standpoint: specific essential anthropological and sociological foundations sustain and govern its discourse – which are assumed, yet not demonstrated. For that reason, the transcendental signified of the UNDP's discourse is formed by three consecutive essentialist assumptions:

Box 1.1 Three consecutive essentialist assumptions

First assumption: human essence

Freedom is the natural, universal and most basic essence of human beings – i.e., what makes us humans. That is why, in the HDRs, individual capabilities are 'the essence of freedom' (UNDP, 1990: 16) and health, knowledge and income (the basic capabilities) are 'the three *essential* elements of human life' (UNDP, 1990: 12, emphasis added).

Second assumption: ideal individuals

The proper unfolding of this essence produces rational, intelligent, skillful and healthy individuals who are morally and politically committed to constructing a peaceful coexistence, and ready to become active agents of human progress.

Third assumption: an ideal society

A society formed by such individuals will reach a civilizational stage in which humankind enjoys plenitude and attains its full potential; human beings achieve a peaceful and stable coexistence; institutions work in a perfect and absolutely rational way; people are free and behave in a moral and politically correct manner; the economy is based on win–win initiatives that benefit everyone; wealth is fairly distributed; international relations are based on respect and mutually beneficial cooperation; humans have a sustainable and respectful relationship with nature; and war, violence and oppression disappear.

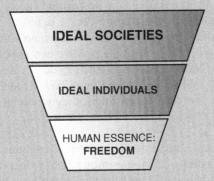

Figure 1.1 Visual representation of the transcendental signified of the UNDP's discourse

These assumptions are a distillation of the highest Humanist and Enlightened ideals that have fed, at least at an ideological and political level, the Western civilizational project during the last few centuries – since Reason replaced God in the search for truth. In ontological terms, the UNDP's transcendental signified revives the theory of the social contract: specifically, the ahistorical and timeless ontological moment in which fully entitled individuals – whose essence is freedom – constitute society. Although these ontological assumptions are strongly sedimented in Western philosophical and political culture – as I show in Chapter 2 – they are not self-evident. However, the reports overlook this debate. They simply assume that these insights are true, and construct the human development framework based on them. In the HDRs, development is understood as the process of *unfolding the human essence* to create ideal individuals and societies:

> The process of development should at least create a conducive environment for people, individually and collectively, to develop their full potential.
>
> (UNDP, 1990: 1)

> (Human development) denotes both the process of widening people's choices and the level of their achieved wellbeing.
>
> (UNDP, 1990: 10)

The UNDP's transcendental signified fulfills what Derrida defines as its most important characteristic: *it is ultimately lacking*. It describes an unreachable and ideal stage that cannot be attained. That is why the entire narration in the HDRs is a description of *the absence* of the ideal horizon defined by the transcendental signified. In other words, the essentialist discourse of the UNDP does not analyse what the world is, but *what it is not*. Let us present two examples. First, key concepts in the UNDP's discourse – such as democracy, human development, freedom and security – are described through their absence, not through their presence. Accordingly, they represent a constant and systematic deferral to the ideal horizon yet to come:

> Democracy and human development (...) are both more a journey than a destination—*a promise* rather than a list. Societies can *be more or less* democratic, just as people can have broader or more constrained choices to lead lives they value. But there is no defined end point. *No society is ever completely democratic or fully developed.* What matters is moving forward, and not slipping back.
>
> (UNDP, 2002: 61, emphasis added).

> Several analysts have attempted rigorous definitions of human security. But *like other fundamental concepts*, such as human freedom, human security is more easily *identified through its absence than its presence.* And most people instinctively understand what security means.
>
> (UNDP, 1994: 23, emphasis added)

These key concepts do not describe a fully present reality; on the contrary, they point far into the future, to the full achievement of the (unreachable) transcendental signified. Their meaning – what people 'instinctively understand' – is an endless interplay between presence and absence. The ideal horizon represents the unreachable future: according to the UNDP, what matters is moving forward towards that goal. That is why the transcendental signified 'is more easily identified through its absence than its presence'.

The second example is the flagship index of the human development paradigm: the Human Development Index (HDI). I started this chapter explaining that, for Laclau, the 20th century began with the 'illusion of transparency'. The HDRs are an exemplary case of this illusion. For the UNDP, these reports reproduce reality and put the reader (the subject) in contact with reality (the object). Statistics play a key role in this process: according to the UNDP, 'human knowledge will progress little unless attempt are made to analyse and measure qualitative phenomena in a scientific, empirical manner' (UNDP, 1992: 28). That is why 'information is demanded that empowers people with facts, not opinion' (UNDP, 2000: 90). However, an analysis of the UNDP's statistical apparatus shows that it is also based on the logic of the presence/absence of the transcendental signified. The HDI describes the absence and the lack of the ideal horizon – not its presence. In other words, the HDI does not measure a reality (allegedly, development). Rather, it measures the absence of an ultimately lacking fullness. It captures lack and deprivation: the distance to the ideal horizon. In 1990, the UNDP presented the HDI as follows:

> The human development index is constructed in three steps. The first step is to define a measure of deprivation that a country suffers in each of the three basic variables – life expectancy, literacy, and (the log of) real GDP per capita. A maximum and a minimum value is determined for each of the three variables given the actual values. The deprivation measure then places a country in the range of zero to one as defined by the difference between the maximum and the minimum.
>
> (UNDP, 1990: 109)

> Placing a country at the appropriate point on each scale and averaging the three scales gives its average *human deprivation index*, which when subtracted from 1 gives the human development index (HDI).
>
> (UNDP, 1990: 13, emphasis added)

The UNDP first measures deprivation, *then* uses the number 1 to translate deprivation into achievement. In the construction of indices, the number 1 (100%) represents fullness: absolute achievement. The UNDP measures deprivation and then contrasts it with the ideal horizon, which is necessarily absent: no country has ever received an HDI of 1. In this sense, it is quite telling that the first time the HDI of every country was ranked and published (UNDP, 1990: 111), the list began with the less developed countries and ended with the more developed ones: Niger was first with a mark of 0.116, Mali second with 0.143, and more than 100 positions below, Japan in the last position with 0.996. It was a list of absence, not presence.

On the basis of this game of presence and absence, the UNDP constructs the binary oppositions that animate the human development discourse (see Figure 1.2). Each pair of terms – for example, modern/traditional, distribution/inequality or health/illness – represents a binary opposition. The privileged term is written in bigger letters. The fact that they form a binary opposition does not mean they are antonyms. It just means that in the UNDP's discourse they represent an antagonistic duality that gives both of them meaning. Following Derrida's understanding of essentialist binary oppositions, it is assumed that the privileged term is closer to the transcendental signified, and the non-privileged one further from this ideal. In other words, the transcendental signified is assumed to be *more (but not totally) present* in the privileged term and *more (but not totally) absent* from the other one. In this way, the transcendental signified governs the discourse from outside and defines the hierarchical organization of each binary opposition. As I explain in Chapter 5, in this discursive context, human development is the empty signifier that symbolizes the movement towards the unreachable ideal horizon. For that reason, each privileged term is systematically related to human development (e.g., democracy, peace, security, human rights, sustainability, equity, distribution, health, knowledge), whereas the non-privileged ones refer to its opposite: underdevelopment (e.g., conflict, totalitarianism, traditional, violence, powerlessness, inequity, poverty and crisis).

Figure 1.2 depicts the cloud of binary oppositions that comprise the UNDP's human development discourse. Following Derrida's perspective on language (*différance*), each term is defined by its relationship to other terms (difference) – for example, the term 'life' is defined by its relationships to death, health, illness and productivity – and systematically refers to the transcendental signified yet to come (deferral). The figure partially betrays Derrida and Laclau's understanding of discourse by presenting in a static form what in practice is an ever-evolving contingent structure. However, as I explain in the following chapters, these binary oppositions and their interrelations remained

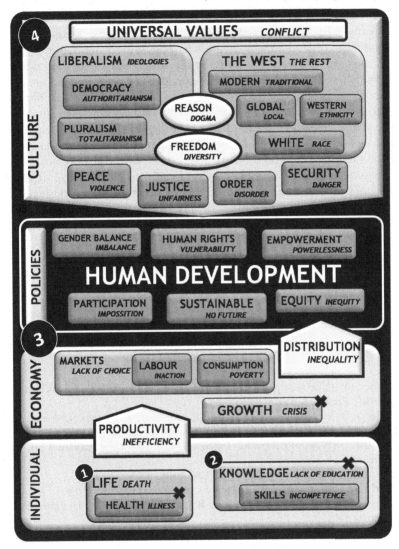

Figure 1.2 The UNDP's human development discourse

unaltered until the 2010s – when the contingency of this discursive structure became apparent and, as I explain in Chapter 5, the human development framework died. In this sense, Figure 1.2 presents the most solid elements of the UNDP's evolving discourse from its inception to its fall, and thus guides my analysis throughout the book.

In Chapter 2, I explain why the figure is divided into four boxes – individual, economy, policies and culture – why these boxes have a hierarchical order, and why each binary opposition is located in a specific box. In Chapter 3, I focus on the lower half of the figure and explain how the UNDP links the individual to human development through its economic discourse. To do so, I focus on two key binary oppositions: productivity/inefficiency and distribution/inequality. In Chapter 4, I analyse the top half of the figure: the UNDP's cultural discourse and its relationship with human development. In this chapter I focus on three important binary oppositions: universal values/conflict, reason/dogma, and freedom/diversity. Finally, in Chapter 5, I explain the political function that this discursive structure played during the 1990s and 2000s, and how, since the mid-2010s, the UNDP's discourse failed to properly carry out this function.

Note

1 Edmund Husserl uses the term 'sedimentation' to evoke the idea of contingent and historically constructed concepts that slowly settle into our understanding of the world and form rock-like assumptions that appear to be self-evident, universal and natural.

References

Bradley, A. (2008) *Derrida's Of Grammatology*, Edinburgh: Edinburgh University Press.

Butler, J., E. Laclau & S. Žižek (2000) *Contingency, Hegemony, Universality: Contemporary Dialogues on the Left*, London: Verso.

Derrida, J. (1978) *Writing and Difference*, Chicago: University of Chicago Press.

Derrida, J. (1981) *Positions*, Chicago: University of Chicago Press.

Derrida, J. (1982) *Margins of Philosophy*, Brighton: Harvester Press.

Derrida, J. (2016) *Of Grammatology*, Baltimore (MD): Johns Hopkins University Press.

Glendinning, S. (2011) *Derrida: A Very Short Introduction*, Oxford: Oxford University Press.

Howarth, D. (2000) *Discourse*, Buckingham: Open University Press.

Howarth, D. (2013) *Poststructuralism and after: Structure, Subjectivity and Power*, Basingstoke: Palgrave Macmillan.

Howarth, D. (2015) *Ernesto Laclau: Post-Marxism, Populism and Critique*, Abingdon: Routledge.

Laclau, E. (1996) *Emancipation(s)*, London: Verso.

Laclau, E. (2000) *Contingency, Hegemony, Universality: Contemporary Dialogues on the Left*, London: Verso.

Laclau, E. (2005) *On Populist Reason*, London: Verso.

Laclau, E. (2014) *The Rhetorical Foundations of Society*, London: Verso.

Laclau, E. & C. Mouffe (1985) *Hegemony and Socialist Strategy*, London: Verso.

Mouffe, C. (2000) *The Democratic Paradox*, London: Verso.

Powell, J. (2006) *Jacques Derrida: A Biography*, London: Continuum.

Saussure, F. (1974) *Course in General Linguistics*, London: Fontana.

Staten, H. (1984) *Wittgenstein and Derrida*, Lincoln (NE): University of Nebraska Press.

UNDP (1990) *Human Development Report. Concept and Measuring of Human Development*. New York: Oxford University Press.

UNDP (1992) *Human Development Report. Global Dimensions of Human Development*, New York: Oxford University Press.

UNDP (1994) *Human Development Report. New Dimensions of Human Security*, New York: Oxford University Press.

UNDP (2000) *Human Development Report. Human Rights and Human Development*, New York: Oxford University Press.

UNDP (2002) *Human Development Report. Deepening Democracy in a Fragmented World*, New York: Oxford University Press.

2 Evolutionism and the matryoshka doll

The measurement of human development should (...) focus on the three essential elements of human life.

(Human Development Report 1990)

Matryoshka dolls nest within each other: each of them holds a smaller matryoshka within, and each of them is held by a larger doll. Only the inner matryoshka is solid and indivisible. They can be displayed in an organized line, from the smallest to the largest, creating a hier-archically organized harmony. Or they can be stacked together to form what appears to be a solid, single doll. The American anthropologist Clifford Geertz explained in 1973 that, for at least two centuries, this is how Western social scientists understood human beings: as comprised of four levels – biological, psychological, social and cultural – each superimposed upon those beneath it and underpinning those above it. Geertz explains that this essentialist understanding of human beings strongly conditioned and limited social sciences.

In this chapter, I look for the genealogical roots of the discursive structure in Figure 1.2. I argue that the United Nations Development Programme's (UNDP's) understanding of people strongly relies on this matryoshka-like essentialist conceptualization. The analysis of the pre-sence of this stratigraphic schema – as Geertz refers to it – in the human development framework shows that the roots of this theoretical assumption go back at least to the 19th-century evolutionist sociologist Herbert Spencer (1820–1903) and transition into the 20th century through the work of another influential evolutionist sociologist, Talcott Parsons (1902–1979). A thorough reading of the Human Development Reports (HDRs) – specifically of the 1990 HDR, in which the UNDP framed the new development paradigm – shows that these reports represent another instalment of this evolutionist perspective. Assessing the influence of the matryoshka-like understanding of human beings and the work of Spencer and Parsons helps us better understand the structure and internal logic of the UNDP's discourse.

Two theoretical challenges

When the UNDP decided in 1989 to start publishing a series of annual reports that would review individual countries' levels of development, former World Bank economist Mahbub ul Haq was placed in charge. The UNDP sought to 'give the organization a new, globally significant, purpose' (Murphy, 2006: 233). Amartya Sen, a professor of economics at Harvard at the time, joined the small group of experts that designed the human development framework in late 1989 and early 1990. The first report was published in May 1990.

Almost two decades later, Sen recalled the project's theoretical challenges (Sen, in Fukuda-Parr & Shiva Kumar, 2009: ix–xii). The team created the new framework as an alternative to the growth-centred paradigm promoted by the Bretton Woods institutions, which had monopolized development debates for more than a decade. According to Sen, this conceptualization of development tended to understand human beings more as a means than an end. Thus the new approach aimed to contribute two alternative perspectives. The first was a clearer and more open comprehension of how (and in what ways) human lives can go much better – what Sen calls 'the evaluative aspect' of development, which requires reflecting on the *meaning of development and social change*. Second, they wanted to overcome the simplistic conceptualization of human beings as mere passive receivers of aid, or as means of economic growth. The team sought to develop a fuller understanding of how this betterment (development) can be achieved by strengthening human agency – what Sen refers to as 'the agency aspect' of development, which requires tackling *the role of human beings in promoting social change* (agency).

The human development framework the team created draws on Sen's capability approach. The main departure from the Bretton Woods growth-centred understanding of development was the framework's focus on freedom: the UNDP strongly linked human development to enhancing individuals' freedom to decide and act. The 1990 HDR was very clear in this respect: 'this Report is about people – and about how development enlarges their choices. (...) Human development is a process of enlarging people's choices' (UNDP, 1990: 1). However, human development was not only a matter of making people freer. The first HDR added two important requisites that differentiated the new framework from other conceptualizations of development

(UNDP, 1990: 10–11). First, it stressed that people should be able to freely participate in the very process of development. They should not be the mere passive beneficiaries of social changes, but also their active agents:

> This Report places people at the centre of human development – as the agents and beneficiaries of the development process. People's needs and interests should guide the direction of development, and people should be fully involved in propelling economic growth and social progress.
>
> (UNDP, 1990: 64)

That is why the human development framework relies on the idea that 'human beings are both the *means* and the *end* of development' (UNDP, 1990: 14): human development not only expands people's ability to choose and act; it also makes them active agents in such a process.

Second, the report explained that in order to truly make people not only the means to development, but also its end, human development had to be understood as a two-step process – what the UNDP calls the *two sides* of human development: (1) the formation of human capabilities and (2) how people make use of these acquired capabilities (UNDP, 1990: 10–11):

> Human development thus concerns more than the formation of human capabilities, such as improved health or knowledge. It also concerns the use of these capabilities, be it for work, leisure or political and cultural activities. And if the scales of human development fail to balance the formation and use of human capabilities, much human potential will be frustrated.
>
> (UNDP, 1990: 1)

Finally, the team decided that the new framework needed a simple index that could draw policy-makers' attention and influence international development debates (Haq, 1995: 25). According to Haq, this was the only way to get the world's attention (Sen, in Weiss et al., 2005: 292). Sen was at first reluctant:

> One slightly negative side of this approach, which relied heavily on public relations, was that in order to win the attention of the public, Mahbub had to simplify tremendously. He went on to do things which were exactly right for his purpose, but also generated a good deal of problems for the intellectual respectability of the

'human development approach'. One of them was his insistence on having one very simple 'Human Development Index' or the HDI.
(Sen, in Weiss et al., 2005: 292)

However, Haq eventually persuaded Sen that 'there was no way of replacing the GNP unless we had another similarly simple index' (Sen, in Weiss et al., 2005: 292). The new index was published in the first HDR. The HDI focused 'on the three essential elements of human life – longevity, knowledge and decent living standards' (UNDP, 1990: 12). The index served as a metric of human development and produced an annual, linear distribution of every country from very high, high, medium, to low human development (in the first reports the distribution was simpler: high, medium and low). Although the human development framework is more than this simple index, the HDI is what 'caught the public's eye and caused the most controversy' after the publication of the first report (Streeten, in Haq, 1995: xi).

Overall, the UNDP responded to the 'evaluative aspect' by identifying development with the enlargement of freedom (capabilities and choices), and to the 'agency aspect' by stressing that people should be the active agents of social change – the means and end of development – which involves both *creating* and *using* capabilities.

Herbert Spencer, Talcott Parsons and the UNDP

In conceptualizing development in this way, the human development framework reproduces and prolongs the way evolutionist sociologists of the 19th and 20th century answered the same two questions: 'what is evolution and social change?' (evaluative aspect) and 'what is the role of the individual in the processes of social change?' (agency aspect). In this section I introduce the key elements of the most influential evolutionist sociologists – Herbert Spencer and Talcott Parsons – and show how their work strongly influenced the UNDP's understanding of development. In Chapter 4, I explain how the UNDP's conceptualization of history and culture parallels another influential evolutionist thinker of the late 20th century, Francis Fukuyama.

Spencer was a prominent English evolutionist anthropologist and sociologist, and an influential Victorian-era liberal political theorist. He developed an all-encompassing evolutionary understanding of reality that was strongly influenced by Auguste Comte's positivism, John Stuart Mill's utilitarian liberalism, and Jean-Baptiste Lamarck's and Charles Darwin's biological evolutionism (Offer, 2010: 27–62). Following Comte's aim to unify all scientific knowledge into a single positivistic system, Spencer sought to build a scientific explanatory framework that could account for the progressive evolution not only of society, but of every knowable reality: from the creation of the solar system to the formation of the human brain, social institutions, moral systems and religious beliefs. To do so, he expanded on Comte's idea that multiple natural universal laws could explain the evolution of both the organic and inorganic realms, and proposed that a single universal law of evolution could explain any observable phenomenon. This implied the natural and necessary transition from a simple, undifferentiated and homogeneous state to a complex, differentiated and heterogeneous one, which more closely integrated several elements:

> Now I propose in the first place to show, that this law of organic evolution is the law of all evolution. Whether it be in the development of the Earth, in the development of Life upon its surface, in the development of Society, of Government, of Manufactures, of Commerce, of Language, Literature, Science, Art, this same advance from the simple to the complex, through successive differentiations, holds uniformly. From the earliest traceable cosmical changes down to the latest results of civilization, we shall find that the transformation of the homogeneous into the heterogeneous, is that in which Evolution essentially consists.
>
> (Spencer, 2009: 148–149)

Within the grand schema dominated by his universal law of evolution, Spencer conceived of society as a natural organism that constantly changes to adapt its structure and processes to the changes in the environment: 'rightly understood, social progress consists in those changes of structure in the social organism' seeking to adapt to the context (Spencer, 2009: 147). Accordingly, a society's evolution could be assessed according to its level (or stage) of adaptation: societies, 'like other organisms, (…) [have] to pass in the course of [their] development through temporary forms' (Spencer, 2009: 256). In this sense, Spencer's conceptualization of social change paralleled Lamarck and Darwin's naturalistic understanding of biological evolution, in which change was driven by an organism's progressive adaptation to the requirements of the changing context. However, Spencer was not always clear whether he believed social evolution followed a Lamarckian logic (based on inheriting acquired habits and the organism's intention to change) or a Darwinian logic (based on natural selection) (Mingardi, 2011: 31).

Since Spencer equated adaptation with progress and evolution, he understood evil as the *lack* of progress and evolution. When applied to political and sociological issues, his universal law of evolution traced a progression from evil to moral perfection: 'all evil results from the non-adaptation of constitution to conditions' (Spencer, 1851: 59). Strongly influenced by the work of John Stuart Mill, Spencer's political theory envisioned the *telos* – the aim, the end, the objective – of humankind as individuals' perfect moral and political adaptation to both external natural and social contexts and to their internal human needs and desires. He described this final stage of this adaptation as follows:

> The establishment of this equilibrium, is the arrival at a state of human nature and social organization, such that the individual has no desires but those which may be satisfied without exceeding his proper sphere of action while society maintains no restraints but those which the individual voluntarily respects. The progressive extension of the liberty of citizens, and the reciprocal removal of political restrictions, are the steps by which we advance towards this state. And the ultimate abolition of all limits to the freedom of each, save those imposed by the like freedom of all, must result from the complete equilibration between man's desires and the conduct necessitated by surrounding conditions.
>
> (Spencer, 2009: 470–471)

According to Spencer, expanding human freedom by progressively extending citizens' liberty would generate a peaceful and harmonious coexistence – a liberal equilibrium in which 'human beings became perfectly adapted to the needs of living in society and (...) spontaneously behave in an ethical manner, that is, in conformity to the law of equal freedom while also showing beneficence towards others' (Taylor, in Francis & Taylor, 2015: 53–54). There is a noteworthy similarity between Spencer's liberal equilibrium and the UNDP's transcendental signified presented in Chapter 1.

Parsons rejected some of the central aspects of Spencer's work – such as positivism and utilitarianism – however, the latter had an important influence on his thinking. Parsons was one of the most influential American sociologists of the 20th century. He was interested in evolution, not *Evolution*, which he labelled as Spencer's God (Gerhardt, 2002: 8). In order to explain evolution in a different way to Spencer, Parsons developed a more voluntarist account of social change, drawing on the work of Max Weber. He also left behind the organic metaphors used in the 19th century to explain evolution, and focused on the systemic character of social relations. The result was his introduction of the novel structural functionalist framework known as 'theory of action' in the late 1930s. It relied on systems theory, which maintained that society was comprised of many internal systems (such as families, enterprises, institutions) and formed a part of larger and more general systems (such as the ecological environment and other societies). Parsons proposed a dynamic sociological framework that defined each part according to its functions, structure and the way it interacted with other parts of the system.

In some respects, Parsons' explanatory schema reproduced some of Spencer's conclusions. For example, Victorian England was for Spencer the best example of satisfactory *social evolution*, as the USA was for Parsons the best example of *evolutionary adaptation* (Parsons, 1977). However, Spencer's explanations relied heavily on the inexorable influence of his proposed universal law, whereas Parsons' structural functionalist schema conceived evolution as a process of adaptation based on the differentiation/integration of new elements (Parsons, 1966: 21). Changes in the environment force the system to create new ways of dealing with problems, so the whole structure evolves to become more complex, and more adapted to the natural and social environment – and, accordingly, more capable of persisting over time. Systems naturally seek stability – a characteristic called homeostasis; this tendency causes societies to evolve into more complex and adapted forms.

One of the most salient aspects of Parsons' work for the current analysis is his interest in agency – an individual's capacity to decide, act and change society. Spencer's focus on the explanatory power of the universal law of evolution led him to reject the idea that individuals had 'any way of forcing the direction or rate of change' (Francis, in Francis & Taylor, 2015: 1). On the contrary, Parsons proposed a new approach to human action, which was influenced by Max Weber's emphasis on the motivational dimension of individual actions, Vilfredo Pareto's analyses of rational action, and Sigmund Freud's analysis of the influence of the superego on people's behaviour (Best, 2015: 121; Gerhardt, 2002: 28, 53). Parsons elaborated a cybernetic explanation of human action, which has important implications for understanding the UNDP's human development framework. He maintained that a system's adaptation and evolution were the result of two inputs: energy and information. Parsons located the individual's action at the nexus of these inputs. On the one hand, the individual has the ability to transform energy and natural resources into practices and institutions that fulfil the needs of the system. On the other hand, the individual behaves according to cultural and religious patterns that normatively condition his or her decisions. Parsons defined action as 'the behavior orientated to the attainment of ends in situations, by means of the normatively regulated expenditure of energy' (Parsons, 1962: 53). From this perspective, the individual's ability to transform energy and information into systemic adaptation was the pivot of his structural functionalist framework: Parsons located individual agency at the core of his evolutionary theoretical framework – hence the name 'theory of action'.

Overall, there are three main parallels in the way Spencer, Parsons and the UNDP answered the questions about development and agency related to both evaluative and agency aspects. First, in relation to the evaluative aspect, all three of them understand that evolution is a matter of adaptation. Spencer draws on Lamarck and Darwin's work to conceptualize adaptation in biological terms, while Parsons explains it in terms of a system's reaction to changes in the environment, using a cybernetic approach that merges energy and information. The UNDP describes development by combining two kinds of adaptation: (1) an individual's adaptation (primarily to the economic system, but also to social institutions), and (2) countries' adaptation to global economic, financial and trade tendencies. The following example illustrates both types of adaptation:

> A key challenge for Africa is to accelerate investment in people: in their nutrition and health (especially that of women and children) and in their education, particularly in science and technology. This could help African countries *adapt* to new technologies and become more productive, creative and enterprising – and start catching up with the rest of the world.
>
> (UNDP, 1992: 40, emphasis added)

In Chapter 3 I focus on how the UNDP conceptualizes this adaptive relationship and how economic institutions mediate the relationship between the individual and human development.

The second parallel, still in relation to the evaluative aspect, is that all three of them assume that there is a universal pattern of evolution that can be used to evaluate how adapted and evolved a particular human group is. For Spencer, this is the universal law of evolution and the achievement of the liberal equilibrium; for Parsons, it is the General System of Action and the cybernetic adaptation of the system to the environment; and for the UNDP it is the human development framework and the attainment of the transcendental signified. In each case, this universal pattern enables the reduction of plurality and complexity to a linear understanding of the evolution of societies. In the case of the UNDP, the capabilities approach contributes a normative and universal standard for comparison that enables: (1) *homogenization and standardization* – the inherent differences and specific characteristics of each group are disregarded and only a set of traits is considered for the evaluation; (2) *comparison* – on the basis of these homogeneous and standard characteristics, human groups can be compared; and (3) *classification* – drawing on an explicit or implicit normative pattern, the comparison allows countries to be ranked according to their level of evolution.[1] The result is the HDI: the statistical tool used by the UNDP to quantify, compare and classify each country's performance; the labels 'very high', 'high', 'medium' and 'low' human development represent the stages of the evolutionary ladder.

Finally, in relation to individual agency in the process of evolution and social change, Spencer did not grant the individual an important role in the evolution of humankind; he focused his attention on the universal law of evolution. However, shifting the focus to individual agency was one of Parsons' most important contributions to the evolutionary tradition: by doing this, he adapted the biology-inspired evolutionist perspective of the 19th century to the general trends in social sciences in the early 20th. As explained above, the human development framework's main contribution in 1990 was a reconceptualization of development in terms of agency and freedom: the UNDP located individuals at the centre of development – as both means and ends – and defined human development as the process of acquiring and using individual capabilities.

There is yet another very important implicit similarity between Spencer and Parsons, which facilitates a more thorough analysis of the evolutionist roots of the human development framework, as well as a better understanding of the essentialist foundations of the UNDP's discourse. This similarity is based on a very specific conceptualization of human beings and their social, political and economic interactions.

Clifford Geertz and the stratigraphic schema

As mentioned in the introduction of this chapter, in *The Interpretation of Cultures* (1973) the anthropologist Clifford Geertz reflected on how the conceptualization of culture influenced the conceptualization of human beings for two centuries (Geertz, 1973: 33). Geertz explains that, in the inquiry about the essential nature of human beings, most thinkers since the Enlightenment have assumed there is a single overall intellectual strategy:

What I will call (…) the 'stratigraphic' conception of the relations between biological, psychological, social, and cultural factors in human life. In this conception, man is a composite of 'levels,' each superimposed upon those beneath it and underpinning those above it. As one analyzes man, one peels off layer after layer, each such layer being complete and irreducible in itself, revealing another, quite different sort of layer underneath. Strip off the motley forms of culture and one finds the structural and functional regularities of social organization. Peel off these in turn and one finds the underlying psychological factors – 'basic needs' or what-have-you – that support and make them possible. Peel off psychological factors and one is left with the biological foundations – anatomical, physiological, neurological – of the whole edifice of human life. (…) Man was a hierarchically stratified animal, a sort of evolutionary deposit, in whose definition each level – organic, psychological, social, and cultural – had an assigned and incontestable place.

(Geertz, 1973: 37–38)

I depict Geertz's explanation in Figure 2.1: the stratigraphic understanding of human beings is a theoretical matryoshka-like anthropology. According to Geertz, this conceptualization had two main benefits for mainstream social sciences during last two centuries. First, once culture, society, psyche and organism were 'converted into separate scientific "levels," complete and autonomous in themselves' the independence of (and articulation between) the established academic disciplines – biology/medicine, psychology, sociology/economics and anthropology – was guaranteed and coordinated (Geertz, 1973: 41). In other words, this structured understanding of human beings respected and reinforced the epistemological and theoretical general framework

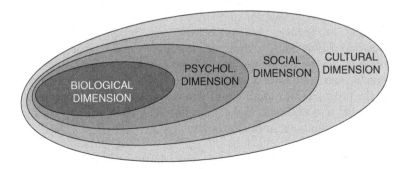

Figure 2.1 Stratigraphic understanding of human beings

of the last two centuries. The second benefit was that this approach enabled a supposedly scientific and hierarchically structured search of the human essence by connecting the allegedly universal findings in the cultural, social and psychological dimensions with certain invariant points of reference in the lower levels. That is to say, any cultural element would be regarded as essential if its relationship with sociological, psychological or biological aspects could be demonstrated. Geertz's criticism of this strategy is that it extended and consolidated 'the notion that the essence of what it means to be human' is most clearly revealed in human features that can be linked to the invariant, universal features in the lower levels, which is a prejudice that 'we are not necessarily obliged to share' (Geertz, 1973: 43). Generally, the American anthropologist criticized the rigid hierarchical organization of the stratigraphic schema and the reduced role that 20th-century academia gave to anthropologists, as the experts on culture – that is to say, the experts on those human issues that doctors, biologists, psychologists, sociologists and economists – could not explain.

The stratigraphic schema described by Geertz remains implicit in how Spencer and Parsons conceptualized and explained human beings. In *First Principles* (1862), Spencer outlined an academic and intellectual project that sought to demonstrate that all scientific knowledge could be gathered and connected under the explanatory umbrella of the universal law of evolution. After an exposition of the ontological and epistemological principles that would sustain the whole explanatory building, he presented the steps of this project as follows (Spencer, 2009: v–x): (1) an explanation of the 'principles of biology', including physics and chemistry and the evolution of life; (2) a review of the 'principles of psychology', which include the mind and general mental phenomena; (3) an analysis of the 'principles of sociology' to understand the evolution of human ideas and feelings within a social environment, and the creation of political and social institutions; and (4) an inquiry into the 'principles of morality' and justice, towards which, according to Spencer, human beings were progressing. Spencer's endeavour plainly follows the stratigraphic schema. Furthermore, his work provides an exemplary case of the search for universal human characteristics that Geertz criticized. For example, Spencer assumed that the principles of morality – in the fourth layer – that were to take humankind to a perfect liberal equilibrium were universal because they had solid foundations in the lower levels:

> [The principles of morality are] generalizations furnished by Biology, Psychology and Sociology, which underlie a true theory of

right living: in other words, the elements of that equilibrium between constitution and conditions of existence, which is at once the moral ideal and the limit towards which we are progressing.

(Spencer, 2009: ix)

Parsons designed a systematic approach to the evolution of social systems called AGIL, which I reproduce in Figure 2.2.

AGIL	
FUNCTIONS	**GENERAL SYSTEM OF ACTION**
<Environment>	*Ultimate Reality*
Latency - Pattern Maintenance	**Cultural System**
Integration	**Social System**
Goal Attainment	**Personality System**
Adaptation	**Behavioral System**
<Environment>	*Physical-Organic Environment*

Figure 2.2 Parsons' systematic approach to the evolution of social systems

AGIL refers to the four functions that, according to Parsons, any society has to fulfil in order to persist over time. *Adaptation* is the proper management of interactions with the surrounding environment; *Goal attainment* is the establishment of future goals that help in taking decisions; *Integration* refers to the harmonization of the group in order to avoid dissemination; and *Latency* (or pattern maintenance) is the maintenance of general patterns that ensure the integration of the group. The AGIL approach assumed that these essential functions were universal and necessary in any society – hunter-gatherers and highly industrialized modern societies alike. For that reason, to carry out these four functions, Parsons suggested that every society was formed by four hierarchically connected subsystems of action: behavioural, personality, social and cultural. Each system specializes in fulfilling its corresponding function in the figure (Parsons, 1966: 7). In this way, Parsons' general System of Action (right column in Figure 2.2) plainly reproduces Geertz's stratigraphic schema. Indeed, this is not a coincidence: Parsons and Geertz worked together at Harvard in the early 1950s, and the critique of the stratigraphic schema represents Geertz's reactions to Parsons' understanding of social sciences.

It is important to stress that both Spencer and Parsons reproduce the four layers of the stratigraphic schema *and their hierarchical organization*: biology first, psychology second, society third and finally culture.

Human development and the stratigraphic schema

The stratigraphic schema is important for our inquiry into the UNDP's discourse because the human development framework and, more generally, the way the organization responded to the theoretical challenges posed by the evaluative and agency aspects, plainly reproduce the schema and its internal hierarchical logic.

Geertz explains that the four layers of the schema represent both the individual and the group: the two internal layers account for the individual (its 'biological and psychological nature') and the two external ones (social and cultural dimensions) represent 'the external situations in which [individuals] live and act' (Geertz, 1973: 41). The UNDP plainly reproduces this individual/group division when it explains that human development entails two sides – one is the creation of capabilities and the other is their use: capabilities are created at the individual level and used at the group level:

> [It is important] to distinguish clearly between two sides of human development. One is the formation of human capabilities, such as improved *health or knowledge*. The other is the use that people make of their acquired capabilities, *for work or leisure*.
>
> (UNDP, 1990: 10–11, emphasis added)

These two sides represent, in reality, a threefold division. When the UNDP explains the basic capabilities that have to be created at the individual level, it systematically reproduces the two internal layers of the stratigraphic schema: *health* [1] is a basic capability because it represents the essence of the biological layer, and *education* [2] represents the basic investment in individuals' psychological development. Then, when the UNDP focuses on the use of these capabilities, it always refers to the individual's ability to participate at the group level [3]: access to the market, political participation and cultural activities. This threefold division, for example, is plainly reproduced in the structure of the HDI:

> This Report suggests that the measurement of human development should for the time being focus on *the three essential elements of human life* – longevity, knowledge and decent living standards.
>
> (UNDP, 1990: 11–12, emphasis added)

Longevity and knowledge refer to the *formation* of human capabilities, and income is a proxy measure for the choices people
have in putting their capabilities to *use*.

(UNDP, 1990: 14, emphasis added)

The three essential elements described by the UNDP echo the three
internal layers of the stratigraphic schema.

It is important to stress that when the UNDP unknowingly reproduces the stratigraphic schema, it faithfully respects the hierarchical
organization of the layers, and the idea that the inner layers underpin
the external ones. For example:

By providing basic health care, adequate nutrition, and nurturing
and stimulation in a caring environment, interventions in early
childhood development help ensure children's progress in primary
school, continuation through secondary school and successful
entry into adulthood and engagement in the workforce.

(UNDP, 2014: 57)

The UNDP assumes that properly developing the first layer of the
schema (health and nutrition as basic elements of the biological layer)
helps properly develop the second layer (primary and secondary
school) to successfully reach the third and fourth layers – to become a
member of society. This hierarchical assumption is implicitly present in
the reports: as illustrated in the quotations cited above, every reference
to individual capabilities systematically mentions health first, then
education and finally social, political, economic and cultural aspects.
Similarly, the visual representation of the HDI follows this hierarchical
structuration (see Figure 2.3), and the statistical tables for the HDI in

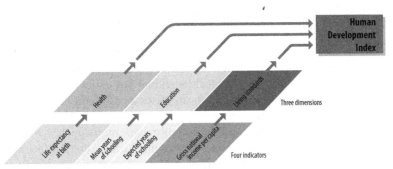

Figure 2.3 HDI components
Source: UNDP, 2010.

any of the 26 HDRs always represent health first, then education and finally income.

The implicit presence of the stratigraphic schema in the human development framework explains why Figure 1.2 (in Chapter 1) is formed by four hierarchically organized sections:

- *The individual.* At the bottom of the figure, numbers 1 and 2 refer to the two inner layers of the schema. These layers constitute the individual's biological dimension (life and health) and psychological abilities (knowledge and skills). These two dimensions account for their basic capabilities: each black 'X' marks one of the sub-indexes of the HDI.
- *Economy.* Above, the economic dimension, formed by markets (both labour and goods/services) and economic growth, is marked with an 'X' because it is the third sub-index of the HDI. According to the UNDP's discourse, a healthy and skilful individual is more productive and performs better in the economic dimension: that is why productivity links the first two boxes. In other words, the individual uses his or her acquired basic capabilities in the economic dimension.
- *Policies.* The UNDP explains that, if economic wealth is properly distributed, new capabilities and opportunities to participate in social and political life emerge. That is why distribution is the link between the second and third sections. The third section is the point at which proper human development – not just economic development – takes place. The number 3 between the second and third sections indicates that together they form the third layer of the stratigraphic schema.
- *Culture.* The fourth layer is cultural. It provides the general information – moral, political and cultural values and principles – that feeds and legitimates the human development process.

As explained in Chapter 1, the transcendental signified of the UNDP's discourse is implicitly present in Figure 1.2 and contributes the overall logic within it. The ideal individual posited by the UNDP is healthy, intelligent and skilled (bottom of the figure) and has no difficulties in applying her capabilities in properly functioning markets. Her high-minded values and solidary commitments motivate her to distribute wealth fairly, so everyone can acquire further capabilities and participate in constructing a better society. Together, the idealized individuals create a society in which people are empowered, human rights are respected, everyone has equal opportunities and humans have a sustainable relationship with the environment. The values that guide these individuals are universal – e.g., peace, justice, order, security – and based on freedom and the use of reason (top part of the figure). As mentioned in Chapter 1, the privileged term in each binary opposition in the figure points to the achievement of the transcendental signified, while the unprivileged terms describe the actual, unsatisfactory world that should be overcome.

Bottom-up: an essentialist and individualist discourse

The logic within the UNDP's discourse (Figure 1.2) follows the cybernetic logic proposed by Parsons. From the bottom up, the energy of the human body rises and animates the economic practices that introduce energy and resources into the human development process. From the top down, the information in the cultural realm channels the bottom-up practices towards human development. In the following two sections, I focus on these two hierarchical logics.

The bottom-up logic is essentialist and individualist: as explained above, development is understood as the unfolding of the human essence, which results first in healthy and educated *individuals*, and then in fair, stable and peaceful *societies*. In other words, the focus is on the individual and her essence. This is not new in development debates, which emerged within a culture of economism, where economic sciences set the theoretical basis of mainstream development thinking (Nederveen, 2001: 67; Stokke, 2009: 40). In this way, the individualistic perspective of the mainstream microeconomic theories from the 18th and 19th centuries – especially those of the Marginal Revolution – transitioned into several economic works that strongly influenced the way development was conceptualized in the 1950s and 1960s – e.g., Joseph Schumpeter's *The Theory of Economic Development* (1911), Alfred Pigou's *The Economics of Welfare* (1920), Arthur Lewis' *The Theory of Economic Growth* (1955) and Walt Rostow's *The Stages of Economic Growth* (1960). Amartya Sen – who was awarded the Nobel Prize in Economic Sciences in 1998 – reproduces this essentialist and individualistic tradition in his capabilities approach. When he explains, for example, that a functioning is what *a person* manages to do or be, and that, accordingly, the capability to function is what *a person* can do or be (Sen, 1987: 7, emphasis added), the bearer of capabilities and the doer of functionings, actions and achievements is the individual. *Then*, after the individual has been constituted, Sen focuses on political and social elements – the context – to explain that the lack of freedom and choices influences the probability and the negative effects of poverty and famines institutions – for example in *Poverty and Famines: An Essay on Entitlement and Deprivation* (1981). When the UNDP explains, for example, that the formation of human capabilities is one side of the human development framework, and that the use people make of their acquired capabilities is the other, the bearer and user of these capabilities is the individual (UNDP, 1990: 10). Hence, the essentialist and individualist assumptions in the human development framework's bottom-up logic have a twofold origin: the stratigraphic schema inherited from evolutionist sociologists, and the capabilities approach's economistic and individualistic foundations.

According to this perspective, transformation can only happen by transforming the constitutive element of social life: the individual. That is why it is *the means* and the end of development. For that reason, the human development framework explains *the development of individuals, not of groups, countries or regions*. When the UNDP affirms that a country is developed, this means that the individuals who comprise that country are developed. When the UNDP affirms that one country is more developed than another, this indicates that, on average, the individuals in the former are more developed that those in the latter. Accordingly, the HDI does not rank countries according to their development; it ranks groups of individuals under the label of a country. That is why the sub-indexes of the HDI – life expectancy at birth, expected years of schooling, mean years of schooling and GNI per capita – systematically refer to individuals: countries have no life expectancy at birth or expected years of schooling. In other words, the HDI does not measure the development of a country, but the development of an average citizen of that country.

When Geertz explains, as mentioned above, that the prejudice that the essence of the individual is revealed in the two lower levels of the stratigraphic schema is something that 'we are not necessarily obliged to share' (Geertz, 1973: 43), he is denouncing the limitations imposed by the essentialist ontology too. A good example of these limitations is the fact that the stratigraphic lens reduces the scope and causes the observer to systematically focus on the same elements. For example, when Geertz, from a critical standpoint, describes each layer of the schema, he precisely describes the HDI: he mentions health and curing procedures to describe the biological layer; educational institutions and personal growth for the psychological one; and trade and the allocation of goods and services for the social layer (Geertz, 1973: 42). Similarly, when Parsons explains the content of each level of the General System of Action, he stresses the importance of health and food at the level of the behavioural organism, of institutionalized literacy for the personality system, and of money and other symbolic representations of exchange and power at the social system level (Parsons, 1966). Furthermore, in *The System of Modern Societies* (1971), Parsons previewed the UNDP's solution to the evaluative aspect. Parsons explains that one of the ways to reconcile equality and competence is through 'the institutionalization of equality of opportunity, so that no citizen shall (...) be barred from equal access to opportunities for performance, as in employment, or opportunities for making effective performance possible, like health and education' (Parsons, 1971: 120). In this sense, the publication of the human development framework in 1990 was not a novel proposal. On the contrary, it was the result of applying the old stratigraphic, essentialist and individualist lens to the global analysis of inequality, poverty and exclusion. In Chapter 3, I focus on this bottom-up logic and I explain the limitations that it generates to tackling inequality problems.

Top-down: secular humanism and belief

The cultural section at the top of Figure 1.2 represents the values that animate the UNDP's discourse and channel the bottom-up practices towards human development. In the evolutionist work of Spencer and Parsons, the fourth layer – the cultural one – plays a special role. For the former, the cultural layer is the field of morality. In evolutionary terms, it is the realm of universal principles and ideals that guide humankind to a liberal equilibrium in which each individual's freedom is equally respected, and where morality and politics merge to enable a peaceful and harmonious coexistence (Spencer, 2009: 470–471). In general terms, Parsons agrees that the fourth layer combines the principles and values that point to the ideal future described by the transcendental signified: for him, the cultural system refers to 'what we ordinarily call moral' (Parsons, 1977: 15). He stresses the legitimizing function that cultural values have in stabilizing the normative order that sustains the social system (Parsons, 1971: 11), and explains that 'the generalization of value systems (...) has been a central factor in the modernization process' (Parsons, 1977: 15). However, we find another noteworthy insight in Parsons' work.

In *Action Theory and the Human Condition* (1978), he reflects on the process of modernization and the concept of secularization, as the transition from religious to secular beliefs. Parsons explains that sociologists generally accepted that this process implied the disposing of transcendental beliefs (religion) for the benefit of empirical and rational argumentation. However, he accepts that 'the other possibility

(...) should not be forgotten, namely that the secular order may change in the direction of closer approximation of the normative models provided by a religion, or by religion more generally' (Parsons, 1978: 240). Rather than a separation from religious beliefs, the second possibility suggests that modernization would represent a secular internalization of transcendental beliefs. Drawing on the second possibility, Parsons makes two contributions that are relevant to the analysis of the UNDP's discourse. First, following Weber, he explains that religious values in Western, modern societies came to be institutionalized, and defined 'the situation for the conduct of members of secular societies' (Parsons, 1978: 241). This process created what he calls 'secular humanism'. It is noteworthy that Parsons' description of the content of secular humanism highlighted the most important elements of the human development framework 12 years before the UNDP elaborated them:

> From the societal point of view, perhaps it can be said that (...) the demand for inclusion of all human classes on a basis of some kind of fundamental equality has become irresistible. From the point of view of the conventional criteria of progress, in spite of the turbulent vicissitudes of recent times (...) the story has been on the whole still one of progress, namely higher levels of welfare, of education, of health and longevity, of access, for the previously disadvantaged classes, to the good things previously monopolized by the privileged.
>
> (Parsons, 1978: 251–252)

The description Parsons presents of secular humanism – progress, equal opportunities, education, health, welfare and longevity – suggests that the human development framework could be considered an example of the institutionalization of religious values described by the American sociologist. Parsons' second contribution explains that the Judeo-Christian religious tradition irrevocably mired man in 'sin and death', yet conceptualized him as 'the image of God' and the 'lord of the Creation'. He concludes:

> Indeed the very center of the constitutive symbolism of Christianity would be meaningless without this duality – to put it in one way, if man were totally 'lost' why should God make his 'only begotten son' a *man* of flesh and blood in order to make human salvation possible?
>
> (Parsons, 1978: 241)

According to Parsons, the dual Christian division – man as sin vs. man as salvation – generated insuperable tensions within its secularized humanist version. Parsons concludes that these tensions 'do not disappear, but come to be restructured; the world as such is in its very nature *never* the transcendently defined ideal' (Parsons, 1978: 241).

Parsons' reflection on the moral principles within the fourth layer of the stratigraphic schema directly points to the reflection that opened this book. The relentless and endless Western quest for a better world on earth is, from this perspective, the secular version of the worldly human struggle to become one with God – i.e., to purify the corrupted and particular nature of human beings and bring it to the realm of universal perfection and absoluteness. This insuperable tension is plainly reproduced by the structure and the internal logic of the UNDP's discourse. The transcendental signified, and the privileged term of each binary opposition in Figure 1.2 point far into the man-as-salvation; whereas the unprivileged term describes the man-as-sin. The former is the telos of development – the realm of the universal truth, absoluteness and perfection; the latter represents underdevelopment – conflict, corruption and particularity. That is why Laclau's question about the relationship between universalism and particularism serves as a proper framework with which to analyse the UNDP's discourse. In Chapter 4, I analyse further the cultural dimension within the UNDP's discourse, and I expose its internal tensions and contradictions.

Note

1 For a further explanation of these three steps, and their similarity with the power technique Michel Foucault called 'the exam' in *Discipline and Punish* (1975), see Telleria, 2015.

References

Best, S. (2015) *Talcott Parsons: Despair and Modernity*, Farnham (UK): Ashgate.

Foucault, M. (1995) *Discipline and Punish*, New York: Vintage Books.

Francis, M. & M.W. Taylor (2015) *Herbert Spencer: Legacies*, Abingdon: Routledge.

Fukuda-Parr, S. & A.K. Shiva Kumar (2009) *Handbook of Human Development*, New Delhi: Oxford University Press.

Geertz, C. (1973) *The Interpretation of Cultures*, New York: Basic Books.

Gerhardt, U. (2002) *Talcott Parsons: An Intellectual Biography*, Cambridge: Cambridge University Press.

Haq, M.U. (1995) *Reflections on Human Development*, Oxford: Oxford University Press.

Lewis, W.A. (2003) *The Theory of Economic Development*, Abingdon: Routledge.

Mingardi, A. (2011) *Herbert Spencer*, London: Continuum.

Murphy, C. (2006) *The United Nations Development Programme: A Better Way?*Cambridge: Cambridge University Press.

Nederveen, J. (2001) *Development Theory: Deconstructions/Reconstructions*, London: Sage.

Offer, J. (2010) *Herbert Spencer and Social Theory*, Basingstoke: Palgrave Macmillan.

Parsons, T. (1962) The law and social control, in W.M. Evan (ed.), *Law and Sociology: Exploratory Essays*, Glencoe (IL): Free Press, pp. 56–72.

Parsons, T. (1966) *Societies: Evolutionary and Comparative Perspectives*, Upper Saddle River (NJ): Prentice-Hall.

Parsons, T. (1971) *The System of Modern Societies*, Upper Saddle River (NJ): Prentice-Hall.

Parsons, T. (1977) *The Evolution of Societies*, Upper Saddle River (NJ): Prentice-Hall.

Parsons, T. (1978) *Action Theory and the Human Condition*, New York: Macmillan.

Pigou, A.C. (1920) *The Economics of Welfare*, London: Macmillan.

Rostow, W. (1960) *The Stages of Economic Growth: A Non-Communist Manifesto*, Cambridge: Cambridge University Press.

Schumpeter, J.A. (1983) *The Theory of Economic Development*, Piscataway (NJ): Transaction Publishers.

Sen, A. (1981) *Poverty and Famines: An Essay on Entitlement and Deprivation*, Oxford: Clarendon Press.

Sen, A. (1987) *Commodities and Capabilities*, New Delhi: Oxford University Press.

Spencer, H. (1851) *Social Statics*, London: John Chapman.

Spencer, H. (2009 [1862]) *First Principles*, Cambridge: Cambridge University Press.

Stokke, O. (2009) *The UN and Development: From Aid to Cooperation*, Bloomington: Indiana University Press.

Telleria, J. (2015) Are we still speaking about development? The human development paradigm of the UNDP as power-knowledge, *Nómadas, Revista de Ciencias Sociales*, 43, 241–251.

UNDP (1990) *Human Development Report. Concept and Measuring of Human Development*. New York: Oxford University Press.

UNDP (1992) *Human Development Report. Global Dimensions of Human Development*, New York: Oxford University Press.

UNDP (2010) *The Real Wealth of Nations: Pathways to Human Development*, New York: Palgrave Macmillan.

UNDP (2014) *Human Development Report. Sustaining Human Progress*, New York: UNDP.

Weiss, T.G., T. Carayannis, L. Emmerij & R. Jolly (2005) *UN Voices: The Struggle for Development and Social Justice*, Bloomington: Indiana University Press.

3 Sisyphus and the mountain called capitalism

> We can redress inequalities if we act now, before imbalances in economic power are politically entrenched.
>
> (*Human Development Report 2019*)

According to Greek mythology, Sisyphus was condemned to roll a huge boulder to the top of a mountain. However, every time he neared the summit, exhausted by the effort, the boulder rolled back down the hill, forcing him to start over again and again. In this chapter, I explain that the limitations generated by the discursive structure and internal logics of the human development framework condemns the United Nations Development Programme (UNDP) to a similar never-ending and repetitive task. Every year, the UNDP publishes a Human Development Report (HDR) analysing global issues of inequality, exclusion and poverty and explaining that enhancing people's capabilities would end these problems. However, the boulder always rolls down again; every report presents new information showing that the world is evolving in the opposite direction and that inequalities have never stopped growing, either within or between countries.

In the first half of this chapter, I illustrate how the UNDP's essentialist and individualist understanding of development sustains its faith in the existence of such a hypothetical virtuous circle that, once activated, would take humankind to higher levels of wellbeing. To do so, I analyse the most important binary oppositions at the bottom of Figure 1.2: productivity/inefficiency and distribution/inequality. In the second half of the chapter, I show that the UNDP's discourse is exhausted: despite abundant evidence to the contrary, the UNDP keeps on insisting, even in 2019, that investing in the capabilities of the individual to increase their productivity is the solution. At the end of the chapter, I argue that the stratigraphic, essentialist and individualistic assumptions of the human development framework trap the UNDP into this pattern of thinking, which glosses over the tensions and contradictions between the ideal *future* world that the UNDP envisions and the *present* global economic system – capitalism.

While Sisyphus climbed the mountain infinite times, the UNDP has only done so 26 times so far. However, it appears to be ready to repeat the task many more times: in 2019, it kept repeating that 'we can redress inequalities *if we act now*' (UNDP, 2019: 14, emphasis added), as if it were the first time anyone had pushed the boulder to the top of the mountain.

The UNDP and the virtuous circle of human development

In *Reflections on Human Development* (1995), Mahbub ul Haq defined the four most important elements of the framework as productivity, equity, sustainability and empowerment (Haq, 1995: 16–20). This insight was included in the 1995 HDR:

> There are four major elements in the concept of human development – productivity, equity, sustainability and empowerment. Through enhanced capabilities, the creativity and productivity of people must be increased so that they become effective agents of growth. Economic growth must be combined with equitable distribution of its benefits. Equitable opportunities must be available both to present and to future generations. And all people, women and men, must be empowered to participate in the design and implementation of key decisions that shape their lives.
>
> (UNDP, 1995: 12)

Figure 3.1 illustrates how these four elements form the backbone of the UNDP's human development framework. According to the UNDP, once this 'virtuous circle' (UNDP, 2003: 69; 2013: 5) is activated, 'it

Figure 3.1 The virtuous circle of the human development framework

can be self-reinforcing, cumulative and resilient' (UNDP, 1991: 69). This virtuous circle forms the lowest part of the schema depicted in Figure 1.2.

This section analyses the steps of this sequence, focusing on the HDRs from the early 1990s. The discussion reveals that this flowchart has structured the human development logic since its inception and remains unaltered.

Due to the essentialist and individualist assumptions of the matryoshka-like conceptualization of human beings, the process starts at the two most basic levels of the stratigraphic schema: the individual's health and education. The most important and repeated idea of the human development framework is that 'a healthy, well-nourished, well-educated and skilled labour force is the best foundation for growth' (UNDP, 1991: 13). The UNDP views the link between basic capabilities (health and education) and productivity and economic growth as 'essential for human development' because it 'expands the material base for the fulfilment of human needs' (UNDP, 1996: 50, 66). That is why, at the beginning of the virtuous logic, investment in people's basic capabilities is a key element:

> Human development is concerned both with developing human capabilities and with using them productively. The former require investments in people, the latter that people contribute to GNP growth and employment. Both sides of the equation are essential.
>
> (UNDP, 1992: 2)

The UNDP is well aware that economic growth, *per se*, does not ensure human development. That is why distribution is another important element of the human development process: 'the best way to promote human development is to increase the national income *and* to ensure a close link between economic growth and human well-being' (UNDP, 1991: 3, emphasis added). Indeed, the idea that 'one of the most pertinent policy issues concerns the exact process through which growth translates, or fails to translate, into human development under different development conditions' (UNDP, 1990: 42) distinguished the UNDP's position from the growth-centred perspective of the Washington Consensus adherents in the early 1990s.

The importance of distribution is inherent to the capabilities approach: only a fair distribution enables transitioning from the enhancement of basic capabilities (health and education) to the achievement of further capabilities that allow people to shape their lives. The UNDP explains:

[The human development approach] accepts the central role of human capital in enhancing human productivity. But it is just as concerned with creating the economic and political environment in which people can expand their human capabilities and use them appropriately. It is also concerned with human choices that go far beyond economic well-being.

(UNDP, 1994: 17)

In other words, without distribution, the human development approach is not very different from the human capital perspective of the growth-centred development adherents concerned only 'with human beings as instruments for furthering commodity production' (UNDP, 1990: 11), which the UNDP strongly rejected in 1990.

Distribution is also important because, for the UNDP, it not only affects present generations (equity), but also future ones (sustainability). Since the birth of the human development framework, the UNDP has defended the position that:

The concept of sustainable development is much broader than the protection of natural resources and the physical environment. (...) Sustainable development therefore must also include the protection of future economic growth and future human development. Any form of debt – financial debt, the debt of human neglect or the debt of environmental degradation – is like borrowing from the next generations.

(UNDP, 1990: 7)

That is why the use of acquired capabilities 'clearly contributes (to human development) when it is as fair to future generations as it is to the present ones' (UNDP, 1998: 1).

According to the UNDP, the virtuous circle closes – becomes self-reinforcing, cumulative and resilient – when fair distribution creates equitable societies where people are empowered and can participate in shaping their own lives and futures. The 1993 HDR explains:

The implications of placing people at the centre of political and economic change are thus profound. (...) They call for nothing less than a revolution in our thinking. This Report touches on only a few aspects of a profound human revolution that makes people's participation the central objective in all parts of life.

(UNDP, 1993: 8)

Participation is the cornerstone of the human development framework because it means that 'people are closely involved in the economic, social, cultural and political processes that affect their lives (and) that people have constant access to decision-making and power' (UNDP, 1993: 21). Participation is essential to making people both the means and end of development:

> Since participation requires increased influence and control, it also demands increased empowerment – in economic, social and political terms. In economic terms, this means being able to engage freely in any economic activity. In social terms, it means being able to join fully in all forms of community life, without regard to religion, colour, sex or race. And in political terms, it means the freedom to choose and change governance at every level, from the presidential palace to the village council.
>
> (UNDP, 1993: 21)

As the UNDP explains, reaching the final steps of the virtuous circle was important for the credibility of the human development framework, because 'the purpose of human development is to increase people's range of choices. If they are not free to make those choices, the entire process becomes a mockery' (UNDP, 1992: 26).

Sisyphus and the vicious circle of inequality

However, since the early 1990s, the UNDP's endeavour has resembled the myth of Sisyphus and the boulder. On the one hand, the UNDP insistently proposed that enhancing people's capabilities would increase productivity, and that proper distribution would ignite the virtuous circle of human development. On the other hand, it reported again and again that the world was advancing in the opposite direction.

In the 1990s, the UNDP warned that 'weak human development is likely to result in low growth, further undermining the prospect of future human development' and that the strength of the virtuous circle depended 'on the strength of each link. Weak links can provoke a vicious circle or at least result in development that is lopsided' (UNDP, 1996: 79). In the 2000s, it repeated that:

> This two-way link between human development and economic growth implies virtuous circles—with good human development promoting economic growth, which in turn advances human development. But it also implies vicious circles—in which poor

human development contributes to economic decline, leading to further deterioration in human development.

(UNDP, 2003: 69)

And in the 2010s, it insisted that 'extreme inequality and the concentration of capabilities and opportunities among a narrow elite are part of a vicious circle' and that 'as inequalities become wider, marginalized and excluded groups face growing deficiencies in opportunities to expand and apply their capabilities and to influence the institutions and policies that determine the subsequent distribution' (UNDP, 2016: 80).

However, for three decades, the UNDP witnessed that the hinge of the virtuous circle was not working: *distribution was not occurring* and, accordingly, inequality was not declining but increasing. The reports broadcast that during this period: access to the labour market, which is essential to start the virtuous circle, remained unequal and exclusionary; the wealth generated through productive capabilities was not redistributed; and the production and consumption trends did not properly consider future generations. In the case of access to the labour market, the HDRs showed that the creation of productive capabilities through health and education was not creating new opportunities for everyone. In 1990, the report affirmed:

> Economic growth has failed to provide enough employment opportunities for the job-seekers of the last three decades. Reliable data on open unemployment do not exist, but it is common knowledge that unemployment and underemployment are extensive in many developing countries.
>
> (UNDP, 1990: 26)

The 2015 report written 25 years later, which focused on the relationship between work and human development, explained:

> Today more than half the world's population is under age 30. These young people are likely to be healthier and better educated than their parents and can take advantage of modern communications technologies and media that enable them to engage more fully in global society. So they have higher work expectations – but many of them cannot find work.
>
> (UNDP, 2015: 63)

The evidence confirmed that the virtuous circle was not being created. It also demonstrated that the lack of distribution was a global tendency that had not changed from the 1960s to the present. The 1992 HDR, for example, introduced its analysis as follows:

> The Report presents a disturbing new analysis of the global distribution of income and opportunities – demonstrating that income disparities have in recent years widened dramatically. In 1960, the richest 20% of the world population had incomes 30 times greater than the poorest 20%. By 1990, the richest 20% were getting 60 times more. And this comparison is based on the distribution between rich and poor countries. Adding the maldistribution within countries, the richest 20% of the world's people get at least 150 times more than the poorest 20%.
>
> (UNDP, 1992: 1)

Fifteen years after the first report, the 2005 HDR explained that 'the world's richest 500 individuals have a combined income greater than that of the poorest 416 million' (UNDP, 2005: 4). The 2015 HDR confirmed that the situation was even graver:

> A small elite takes a large share of global wealth. The richest 1 percent held 48 percent of global wealth in 2014, a share projected to be more than 50 percent in 2016. Around 80 percent of the world's people have just 6 percent of global wealth (...). Indeed, just 80 individuals together have as much wealth as the world's poorest 3.5 billion people. Such inequality has become a serious problem – both for economic efficiency and for social stability.
>
> (UNDP, 2015: 65)

Finally, the reports showed that the evolution of sustainability – distribution between different generations – was similar. The 1992 HDR explained that the early 1990s trend was unsustainable:

> Current consumption can not be financed by incurring economic debts that others must repay in the future. Investment must be made in the health and education of today's population so as not to create a social debt for future generations. And natural resources must be used in ways that do not create ecological debts by overexploiting the carrying and productive capacity of the earth.
>
> (UNDP, 1992: 17)

The 1998 HDR focused on the relationship between human development and consumption, and confirmed that the trend had not changed:

The inequities of today are so great that sustaining the present patterns of development and consumption would mean perpetuating similar inequities for future generations. Development and consumption patterns that perpetuate today's inequities are neither sustainable nor worth sustaining.

(UNDP, 1998: 39)

And the 2011 HDR, which focused on sustainability and equity, explains that 'income inequality has worsened, and production and consumption patterns, especially in rich countries, seem to be unsustainable' (UNDP, 2011: 23). The report concludes:

The big message from the ecological footprint is that patterns of consumption and production are unsustainable at the global level and imbalanced regionally. And the situation is worsening, especially in very high HDI countries.

(UNDP, 2011: 25)

The 2019 HDR focused on inequality. The report opened with a straight and shattering statement that put the final nail in the coffin: 'Inequalities. The evidence is everywhere' (UNDP, 2019: 1).

An exhausted discourse

The analysis of the UNDP's reaction shows that the human development framework had very little capacity to rearticulate its discourse and adapt its perspective and advice to this negative evolution. For three decades, the UNDP kept rigidly focusing on creating basic capabilities and affirming that productivity would bring about the needed changes, at the expense of a more profound analysis of the problem of distribution. During the 2000s the UNDP insisted that 'if governments fail to invest adequately in the health and education of their people, economic growth will eventually peter out because of an insufficient number of healthy, skilled workers' (UNDP, 2003: 16). And, in the 2010s, the message did not change:

Pro-poor policies and significant investments in people's capabilities – through a focus on education, nutrition and health, and employment skills – can expand access to decent work and provide for sustained progress.

(UNDP, 2013: iv)

The exhaustion and rigidity of the UNDP's discourse reached its peak in the 2019 report. Although the evidence showed for three decades that expanding access to labour markets was not reducing inequality, the 2019 HDR stressed the importance of productivity, not distribution. As mentioned above, the report focuses on inequalities in human development and how to deactivate the vicious cycle of inequality that creates what the report calls 'the inequality trap' (UNDP, 2019: 12). In chapter 1, the UNDP explains that the problem of inequality is even graver than previously reported. Inequality is not only growing in relation to the capabilities and opportunities for participation and empowerment – at the end of the virtuous circle – due to the lack of adequate mechanisms for redistribution; it is also increasing with regards to access to the productive capabilities that activate the process of human development – at the starting point of the virtuous circle. The report explains that inequality is growing at the level of enhanced capabilities (such as access to quality health, education and modern technologies) (UNDP, 2019: 33), and that inequalities in basic capabilities (such as early child survival and primary school) are falling but remain high (UNDP, 2019: 223). Thus the report acknowledges that, three decades later, the problem is not how to transition from one side of human development (creation of productive capabilities) to the other (use of productive capabilities to unleash further capabilities and opportunities): in 2019, the problem is that inequality is growing even in access to productive capabilities.

It is therefore quite surprising that the 2019 HDR's main proposal to overcome this problem is … increasing productivity:

> Nothing is inevitable about many of the most pernicious inequalities in human development. This is the single most important message of this Report. Every society has choices about the levels and kinds of inequalities it tolerates. Effective action must identify drivers of inequality, which are likely complex and multifaceted, often related to prevailing power structures that the people currently holding sway may not wish to change.
>
> But what to do? Much can be done to redress inequalities in human development with a dual policy objective. First is to accelerate convergence in basic capabilities while reversing divergences in enhanced capabilities and eliminating gender – and other group-based (or horizontal) inequalities. Second, to jointly advance equity and efficiency in markets, *increasing productivity* that translates into widely shared growing incomes – redressing income inequality. The two sets of policies are interdependent, with those

that advance capabilities beyond income often requiring resources to fund public health or education, which are financed by taxes. And the overall resources available are, in turn, *linked to productivity, which is linked in part to people's capabilities.* The two sets of policies can thus work together in a virtuous policy cycle.

(UNDP, 2019: 14–15, emphasis added)

Three aspects demonstrate the inability of the exhausted discourse of the UNDP to tackle real ongoing problems. First, its proposed solution focuses, once again, on increasing productivity rather than redistribution. In other words, the UNDP's faith in the virtuous circle remains untouched, which is why it insists that investing in productivity and efficiency will solve the problem. It still believes there is a natural and virtuous link between economic growth, productivity and human development. The report presents very weak evidence that increasing productivity may result in better income distribution (UNDP, 2019: 233): two analyses conducted by the Human Development Report Office entitled 'Higher labour productivity is associated with a lower concentration of labour income at the top' (Figure 7.2) and 'The relationship between labour productivity and concentration of labour income appears to hold over time at most levels of human development' (Figure 7.3). However, the UNDP acknowledges that the analysis backing this idea is based on only 94 countries and that it might not be definitive 'because this evidence does not indicate the direction of causality' between productivity and income distribution (UNDP, 2019: 233). In any case, this evidence is enough for the UNDP to conclude that 'policies that improve the functioning of markets are thus crucial to increase productivity, also determining the distribution of income' (UNDP, 2019: 234), which leads to the next aspect.

Second, when the UNDP focuses on the next steps of the virtuous circle – the redistributive side – it mentions taxes. However, it is just a mention: redistribution did not occur over a 30-year period and the UNDP does not explain how to make it happen. Indeed, it is very telling that, as mentioned in the paragraph above, the UNDP articulates its redistributive strategy *in relation to markets*:

What to do? The approach proposed in this Report outlines policies to redress inequalities in human development within a framework that links the expansion and distribution of both capabilities and income. The options span premarket, in-market and postmarket policies.

(UNDP, 2019: 4)

In terms of discursive articulation, the redistribution strategies are centred around markets: policies adapt and are described as 'pre-', 'in-' or 'post-' markets. In chapter 7 of the HDR, the UNDP reviews the basics of tax policies: premarket policies are designed to affect people before they become active in the economy, in-market policies regulate the market dynamics, and post-market policies aim to alter the market distribution of income and opportunities. However, this theory was already known in the early 1990s: indeed, the 1991 HDR focused on how to finance development and widely reflected on how taxes could increase public resources and regulate markets. The problem is that, in three decades, none of these sound theoretical proposals were properly and globally implemented and inequality increased. An analysis of why these measures were not implemented would probably be more useful than reviewing the basics of tax policies; however, the UNDP does not research further, which takes us to the third aspect.

Finally, the UNDP affirms that effective action must identify the drivers of inequality, and stresses that they are 'often related to prevailing power structures that the people currently holding sway may not wish to change'. It is positive that the UNDP mentions these structures. However, it is very disappointing that the report only lightly scratches the surface and quickly shies away. Chapter 7 briefly reflects on the declining influence of labour unions and their relationship to inequality (a total of 115 words!) and on the practices in labour markets that do not respect human rights (a total of 29 words!). The report then turns the reflection from power issues towards its comfort zone – the productivity side. It asks:

> But beyond eradicating those practices [that do not respect human rights], how can in-market policies contribute to a fairer distribution of incomes *without hurting incentives for productivity*?
>
> (UNDP, 2019: 234, emphasis added)

Productivity and the instrumental reason

The mantra-like insistence that productivity will solve the problem of inequality takes the UNDP's position close to the growth-centred development strategies that it strongly criticized in the early 1990s:

> Theories of human capital formation and human resource development view human beings *primarily as means* rather than as ends. They are concerned only with the supply side – with *human beings as instruments* for furthering commodity production. True, there is

a connection, for human beings are the active agents of all production. But human beings are more than capital goods for commodity production. They are also the ultimate ends and beneficiaries of this process. Thus, the concept of human capital formation (or human resource development) captures *only one side of human development*, not its whole.

(UNDP, 1990: 11, emphasis added)

At some points, this instrumental view of human beings reaches obscene levels. For example, the 1996 HDR focused on the relationship between human development and economic growth:

Some of the clearest economic benefits of human development arise from making workers, especially poorer workers, more productive by improving their nutrition, health and education. (...) Studies indicate that an increased calorie intake can lead to gains in labour productivity of up to 47% (...). Research suggests that increasing the labour force's average education by one year raises GDP by 9%. But this holds only for the first three years of extra education. After that, the returns to each additional year diminish to around 4% of GDP.

(UNDP, 1996: 76)

Why did the UNDP keep on insisting that productivity is the solution? Why did it end up reproducing the instrumental way to understand human beings that it aimed to overcome? In the next section, I explain the discursive limitations that have prevented the UNDP from understanding the inequality problem in a different way and proposing alternative solutions. However, to properly explain these limitations, I first need to briefly explain some key insights from the work of Max Horkheimer.

In *Eclipse of Reason* (1947), Horkheimer reflects on the profound economic, social and political transformations during the 19th and early 20th centuries' industrialization processes, and explains the rise and consolidation of what he calls 'instrumental reason'. He explains that this type of reason is concerned solely with how to manage the means and resources to achieve an end, that is to say, 'with the adequacy of procedures for purposes more or less taken for granted and supposedly self-explanatory' (Horkheimer 1947: 3). Accordingly, instrumental reason attaches little importance to the question of whether the purposes as such are reasonable. Horkheimer affirms that, in the competitive environment of industrialization, instrumental reason acquired a hegemonic and monopolistic position. Efficiency and pro-ductivity – the optimal use of the means, given a goal – became central economic, social and political features. He explains that since the Enlightenment, and especially during the process of industrialization, this reason became synonymous with 'common sense' (Horkheimer, 1947: 24).

Horkheimer highlights two important consequences of the rise and consolidation of instrumental reason. The first is 'the total transfor-mation of each and every realm of being into a field of means' (Hor-kheimer, 1947: 93). Under the rule of instrumental reason, every resource was understood in terms of optimization and efficiency – including human beings.

> Domination of nature involves domination of man. (...) What is usually indicated as a goal – the happiness of the individual, health, and wealth – gains its significance exclusively from its functional potentiality. These terms designate favourable condi-tions for intellectual and material production.
>
> (Horkheimer, 1947: 93)

The second consequence of instrumental reason is that 'the idea of self-interest gradually gained the upper hand and finally suppressed the other motives considered fundamental to the functioning of society' (Horkheimer, 1947: 19). Justice, equality, happiness and democracy, once thought of as expressions of the universal principles of humanity, were soon reduced to the principle of self-interest (-Horkheimer, 1947: 20).

> One factor in civilization might be described as the gradual repla-cement of natural selection by rational action. Survival or, let us say, success depends upon the adaptability of the individual to the pressures that society brings to bear on him. To survive, man transforms himself into an apparatus that responds at every moment with just the appropriate reaction to the baffling and dif-ficult situations that make up his life. Everyone must be ready to meet any situation.
>
> (Horkheimer, 1947: 95)

The more that instrumental reason dominated the means, the more dominated human beings became: 'the self-renunciation of the indivi-dual in industrialist society has no goal transcending industrialist society' (Horkheimer, 1947: 94). In the competitive environment of industrialization, efficiency and productivity – for their own sakes – became the only goals. Self-interest was elevated to the only and all-encompassing reason, while adaptation and self-preservation became the only aim of life (Horkheimer, 1947: 97).

Fifty years before the UNDP, Horkheimer articulated what the UNDP witnessed and reported between 1990 and 2019. The 1994 HDR warned that the human capital approach – which was concerned with individuals as instruments for furthering production – might prove Horkheimer right:

> Bestowing value on a human life only to the extent that it produces profits – the 'human capital' approach – has obvious dangers. In its extreme form, it can easily lead to slave labour camps, forced child labour and the exploitation of workers by management – as during the industrial revolution.
>
> (UNDP, 1994: 17)

However, two decades later, the UNDP could only report the materialization of Horkheimer's worst-case scenario:

> Globalization has not delivered the expected shared prosperity. Unskilled workers lost jobs in many economies, and manufacturing jobs disappeared. *Productivity* may have increased, but this did not always translate into higher wages, and the *inequality* in pay between unskilled and highly skilled labour has widened considerably.
>
> (UNDP, 2016: 35, emphasis added)

As Horkheimer foretold, the individual became trapped in the vicious circle of the means: what the UNDP defines as the inequality trap.

A mountain called capitalism

Horkheimer precisely describes the construction and consolidation of the 19th and 20th centuries' bourgeois ideology that championed competition and liberal capitalism – of which Herbert Spencer's work is a paradigmatic example.[1] It understood the individual as a surviving social being, constantly adapting to the pressure of competition, whose only motivations must necessarily be self-preservation and self-interest:

> Individualism is the very heart of the theory and practice of bourgeois liberalism, which sees society as progressing through the

automatic interaction of divergent interests in a free market. The individual could maintain himself as a social being only by pursuing his own long-term interests at the expense of ephemeral immediate gratifications.

(Horkheimer, 1947: 138)

According to the analysis in this book, this is the ideology that the UNDP subtly reproduces. The human development discourse focuses on individual capabilities and productivity: the healthier and more educated an individual is, the better he can compete in the labour market and the more he contributes to economic growth. When Horkheimer explains that one factor in civilization might be described as the gradual replacement of natural selection with rational action, he refers to the changes in evolutionist social sciences in the first half of the 20th century, when Darwinian approaches (Spencer) turned into modernization theories (Parsons). Regardless of these changes, Horkheimer continues, the basic assumption remained the same: an individual's survival or success depends on their ability to adapt to the pressures of society. The stratigraphic understanding of human beings was created on the basis of conceptualizing life as self-preservation, adaptation and evolution. That is why Geertz explains that the stratigraphic schema understands human beings as 'a sort of evolutionary deposit' in which each layer of the schema – biological, rational, social and cultural – underpins the next: only a healthy and intelligent/educated individual can succeed in the collective – social, political and economic – realm. That is why the virtuous circle of human development can only start by making the individual more capable of adapting and surviving – i.e., by investing in health and education.

Within this ideology, a better society can be constructed via individual interest and unrestricted competition:

> The bourgeois individual did not necessarily see himself as opposed to the collectivity, but believed or was prevailed upon to believe himself to be a member of a society that could achieve the highest degree of harmony only through the unrestricted competition of individual interests.
>
> (Horkheimer, 1947: 139)

The conviction that society can achieve greater harmony (and get closer to the ideal horizon described by the transcendental signified) through competition, adaptation, survival and individual interest requires an essentialist understanding of society. On the contrary, the rejection of the existence of a universal and essential basis, and the assumption that the principles, interests, motivations, and objectives of any individual or group are contingent and historically located constructions, generates a very different scenario, which is much closer to the world that even the HDRs describe. In other words, only within an essentialist perspective is it possible to argue that self-interest and competition will generate a harmonious equilibrium. That is the case of the UNDP's understanding of development: the activation of the virtuous circle requires investing in the individual's ability to participate in economic activities – that is to say, to compete in markets. Amartya Sen warned in the early 1990s that markets and competition may generate Pareto optimality – i.e., a situation where no individual can be better off without making another individual worse off – but *not a fair distribution of capabilities and opportunities* (Sen, 1993). However, the UNDP overlooked distribution and insisted that productivity would solve inequality issues.

It is very telling that, in 26 reports on poverty, exclusion and inequality, the text of the UNDP's reports mentions capitalism less than 30 times,[2] as if it were an alien concept with little relation to underdevelopment and the lack of distribution. It is hard to imagine a historian writing in 2100 *without* using this word to reflect on the 1990–2020 period. Surprisingly, the UNDP addresses current social, economic and political issues without mentioning it. This is probably why Sisyphus keeps pushing the boulder upwards again and again: he does not know the name of the mountain. I focus on the surprising absence of this term in Chapter 5, where I analyse the political function of the HDRs.

Notes

1 For a further analysis of the instrumental reason in the UNDP's discourse, see Telleria 2014.
2 Quick estimation: (26 reports) × (150–200 pages each) × (500–600 words/page) = nearly 2.5 million words.

References

Haq, M.U. (1995) *Reflections on Human Development*, Oxford: Oxford University Press.
Horkheimer, M. (1947) *Eclipse of Reason*, New York: Oxford University Press.
Sen, A. (1993) Markets and freedoms: achievements and limitations of the market mechanism in promoting individual freedoms, *Oxford Economic Papers*, New Series, 45 (4), 519–541.

Telleria, J. (2014) Two discourses of human development: the contradictions of the UNDP, *Aposta, Revista de Ciencias Sociales*, 63, 1–33.

UNDP (1990) *Human Development Report. Concept and Measuring of Human Development*. New York: Oxford University Press.

UNDP (1991) *Human Development Report. Financing Human Development*, New York: Oxford University Press.

UNDP (1992) *Human Development Report. Global Dimensions of Human Development*, New York: Oxford University Press.

UNDP (1993) *Human Development Report. Peoples' Participation*, New York: Oxford University Press.

UNDP (1994) *Human Development Report. New Dimensions of Human Security*, New York: Oxford University Press.

UNDP (1995) *Human Development Report. Gender and Human Development*, New York: Oxford University Press.

UNDP (1996) *Human Development Report. Economic Growth and Human Development*, New York: Oxford University Press.

UNDP (1998) *Human Development Report. Consumption for Human Development*, New York: Oxford University Press.

UNDP (2003) *Human Development Report. Millennium Development Goals: A Compact among Nations to End Human Poverty*, New York: Oxford University Press.

UNDP (2005) *Human Development Report. International Cooperation at a Crossroad: Aid, Trade and Security in an Unequal World*, New York: UNDP.

UNDP (2011) *Human Development Report. Sustainability and Equity: A Better Future for All*, New York: Palgrave Macmillan.

UNDP (2013) *Human Development Report. The Rise of the South*, New York: UNDP.

UNDP (2015) *Human Development Report. Work for Human Development*, New York: UNDP.

UNDP (2016) *Human Development Report. Human Development for Everyone*, New York: UNDP.

UNDP (2019) *Human Development Report. Beyond Income, Beyond Averages, Beyond Today: Inequalities in Human Development in the 21st Century*, New York: UNDP.

4   We are the champions

These are the reminders of the triumph of the human spirit.
(Human Development Report 1990)

One wonders if gathering 70,000 people in London – capital of the former British Empire – in 1985 to dedicate a song to the people suffering from the famine in Ethiopia, and chanting *'it's been no bed of roses ... no pleasure cruise ... no time for losers, 'cause we are the champions of the world'* was a good idea. In any case, Queen's performance at the 'Live Aid' concert at Wembley Stadium became an iconic cultural moment of the 1980s. Perhaps Francis Fukuyama was inspired by this song when he wrote *The End of History and the Last Man* (1992). He maintains that the liberal and capitalist West is the winner of the historical conflictual struggle, and the only human group to have reached the post-historical civilizational stage; everyone else lives in 'backward, Third World countr(ies) that represent, in effect, an earlier age of mankind' (Fukuyama, 1992: 130). In this chapter, I show that the United Nations Development Programme (UNDP) parallels Fukuyama's understanding of history and culture, and constructs an identity discourse that presents the liberal West as the example of stability and peace for the rest of the world. In this way, the HDRs project the idealized 19th-century representation of human beings and society onto the future: the liberal West is portrayed as the head of the arrow of human evolution. At the end of the chapter, I show that this symbolic representation of history creates an uneasy contradiction for the UNDP: on the one hand, the UNDP adopts a politically correct position and affirms that diversity is positively linked to human development; on the other hand, it prioritizes Western liberalism at the expense of alternative ways of understanding society and human beings.

The chapter focuses on three important binary oppositions in the UNDP's discourse (Figure 1.2): universal values/conflict, reason/ dogma, and freedom/diversity. The critical analysis of these opposi- tions shows that the human development framework grants a privi- leged position to the West, which is portrayed as the expression of the universal.

What does culture mean for the UNDP?

In Chapters 2 and 3, I explained that the capabilities approach of the UNDP and the Human Development Index (HDI) are implicitly based on the stratigraphic schema. The UNDP focuses on the biological and rational-psychological dimensions of the individual (the inner two layers) and on how the individual uses his or her acquired capabilities at the social level (the third layer). However, it neglects the fourth layer (culture) – for example, in the construction of the HDI:

> The HDI – though much broader than GNP – should still be regarded as a partial measure of human progress. It should thus be supplemented by other qualitative and quantitative studies of aspects of human progress – for example, political freedom, *cul- tural progress* or improved physical environment – until a way is found to incorporate these dimensions into the HDI.
>
> (UNDP, 1995: 111, emphasis added)

In this chapter, I focus on how the UNDP articulates culture and diversity within the human development paradigm. Culture is an uneasy and tricky concept that the UNDP tends to avoid: it is a slip- pery slope that exposes the internal tensions and contradictions within the human development framework. The 2004 HDR, for example, focused on cultural diversity and development and struggled to articu- late, in a politically correct way, culture and diversity within the human development framework.

The question is how the UNDP understands culture. Seeking an answer to this question is frustrating in the short term, but very fruitful in the mid-term. It is frustrating for two reasons. First, the UNDP does not have a clear idea of what culture is. The HDRs treat the concept as both everything and nothing, using it to refer to communication and expression, such as language, rituals, art, music, dance, literature, storytelling; objects, artefacts, furnishings, clothing, architecture; values, principles, norms, attitudes; habits, traditions, inherited knowl- edge and techniques; mythology and beliefs; and so on. Democracy, a technique to grind grain, Shakespeare's work, and attitudes to foreign people are all considered cultural in the HDRs (Telleria, 2015). However, not even anthropologists, sociologists and philosophers agree on what culture is. Raymond Williams, in his work *Keywords: A Vocabulary of Culture and Society* (1985: 87), starts his explanation of 'culture' by affirming that '(it) is one of the two or three most complicated words in the English language'. Second, the question of how the UNDP understands culture is frustrating because this ambiguous approach to such a central concept in human and social issues produces incoherence and contradictions. For example, in the 2004 HDR, the UNDP affirms:

> Proponents of cultural determinism often label large parts of the world as simply 'African' or 'Islamic'. But culture is not a homogeneous attribute. There are huge variations in language, religion, literature, art and living styles within the same cultural 'group'.
>
> (UNDP, 2004: 38)

After establishing a coherent criterion to properly reflect on culture, the next page of the report says that 'explaining growth rates, for example, economic policy, geography and the burden of disease were all found to be highly relevant. Cultural factors – such as whether a society is Hindu or Muslim – were found to be insignificant' (UNDP 2004: 39). On page 38 'Islamic' is not a good way to refer to a group because culture is a heterogeneous attribute; however, on page 39 Hindu and Muslim are explanatory cultural factors of societies. If we ask, then, whether religion is cultural or not, more incoherence emerges in the same report, which was touted as being sensitive to cultural issues. On the one hand, the UNDP explains that 'finding answers to the old questions of how best to manage and mitigate conflict over language, religion, culture and ethnicity has taken on renewed importance' (UNDP 2004: v). From this we could conclude that religion is not cultural, since they seem to be independent and mutually exclusive dimensions. On the other hand, a few pages later the report affirms that 'identities based on common cultural characteristics, such as religion, language or ethnicity, appear to promote stronger loyalty among group members than identities based on other characteristics' (UNDP, 2004: 42). In this case religion, as well as language and ethnicity, are considered cultural. These contradictions are even more abundant if we compare different reports. For example, in the 2002 HDR, culture is an important factor for the success of democracy: 'it will not thrive without the spread of democratic culture – of values and principles that guide the behaviour of individuals and groups' (UNDP, 2002: 61). Yet the 2004 HDR disparages the same idea as deterministic and reductionist:

> Cultural determinism – the idea that a group's culture explains economic performance and the advance of democracy – as an obstacle or a facilitator, has enormous intuitive appeal. But these theories are not supported by econometric analysis or history.
>
> (UNDP, 2004: 5)

The 2002 HDR asserts that cultural factors explain the advance of democracy, while the 2004 issue of the report explicitly rejects this idea.

To turn this initial frustration into a fruitful inquiry, we need to reword the question to adapt it to the relational discursive framework presented in Chapter 1. Instead of posing the question in essentialist terms – what *is* culture? – in the following I ask relational questions: how is culture articulated in the UNDP's discursive structure? What is the discursive function of the term 'culture' in the human development framework? What are the binary oppositions that make this term meaningful in the HDRs? What is the relation between culture, human development and the transcendental signified?

Capitalism, liberal democracy and its others

In answering these questions, the UNDP parallels Francis Fukuyama's understanding of culture and history in *The End of History and the Last Man* (1992), which was based on a similarly titled 1989 article. Fukuyama's work is the late-20th century version of Spencer and Parsons' evolutionary theories of the late 19th and mid-20th centuries, respectively. In general terms, Fukuyama (1992: 48) defends the idea that 'there is a fundamental process at work that dictates a common evolutionary pattern for all human societies –in short, something like a Universal History of mankind in the direction of liberal democracy'. According to Fukuyama, such a fundamental process follows Hegel's dialectical explanation of evolution and change, where 'history proceeds through a continual process of conflict, wherein systems of thought as well as political systems collide and fall apart from their own internal contradictions'. Then, 'less contradictory and therefore higher ones' rise anew (Fukuyama, 1992: 60).

In this section, I focus on four key aspects of Fukuyama's approach to culture and history, which, as I explain in the following sections, the UNDP's human development framework reproduces in the HDRs.

First, universal evolution is driven by universal principles and brings humans to an ideal liberal society. In this sense, Fukuyama echoes Spencer and Parsons' assumption that moral and political principles lead the way to a more adapted and better society. Fukuyama is aware that liberal societies are not perfect in practice. However, he asserts that no alternative set of values and principles can compete in terms of legitimacy with those that underpin liberalism: 'what is emerging victorious (…) is not so much liberal practice, as the liberal *idea*', because 'for a very large part of the world, there is now no ideology with pretensions to universality that is in a position to challenge liberal democracy' (Fukuyama, 1992: 45).

For Fukuyama, liberalism is not simply one of many political ideologies; it is the set of principles and values that represents the essential nature of human beings: they 'are not accidents or the results of ethnocentric prejudice, but are in fact discoveries about the nature of man as man' (Fukuyama, 1992: 51).

Second, Western liberal and capitalist societies are the end of history: a civilizational stage at which conflict and fundamental contradictions disappear. These societies are, for Fukuyama, the point at which humankind reaches a stable stage of civilization:

> The fullest embodiment of the principles of the French Revolution were (…) the countries of postwar Western Europe, that is, those capitalist democracies that had achieved a high degree of material abundance and political stability. For these were societies with no fundamental 'contradictions' remaining.
>
> (Fukuyama, 1992: 67)

In this way, Fukuyama distinguishes between the liberal West and its history. He argued that the violent conflicts the West has experienced since the Enlightenment – such as the Second World War and the communist revolutions of the 20th century – represent the final throes of the historical clash of ideologies in the universal evolution towards liberal capitalism:

> The Russian and Chinese revolutions and the Nazi conquests during the Second World War saw the return, in a magnified form, of the kind of brutality that characterized the religious wars of the sixteenth century, for what was at stake was not just territory and resources, but the value systems and ways of life of entire populations. On the other hand, the violence of those ideologically driven conflicts and their terrible outcomes had a devastating effect on the

self-confidence of liberal democracies, whose isolation in a world of totalitarian and authoritarian regimes led to serious doubts about the universality of liberal notions of right.

(Fukuyama, 1992: 11–12)

However, for Fukuyama, the end of the Cold War demonstrated that these liberal notions of 'right' were the expression of human nature: for him, Nazis and communists are those 'other' Westerners left behind in the evolution of universal history.

Third, after the Cold War, the world was divided into two groups of societies: those that reached the end of history and those that did not. In the present and going forward, Fukuyama envisions a dual division of the world between the capitalist, liberal West and the rest of the world. The former is at a post-political civilizational stage in which ideological conflicts and essential contradictions disappear; the latter remains mired in conflict:

> For the foreseeable future, the world will be divided between a posthistorical part, and a part that is still stuck in history. Within the post-historical world, the chief axis of interaction between states would be economic, and the old rules of power politics would have decreasing relevance. (...) On the other hand, the historical world would still be riven with a variety of religious, national, and ideological conflicts depending on the stage of development of the particular countries concerned.

(Fukuyama, 1992: 276)

Fourth, there is a struggle between liberalism and cultural diversity; however, universal evolution will fundamentally homogenize the world. Since the values and principles of the liberal project are not an ethnocentric position, but are instead derived from the discoveries of the true and essential nature of man, Fukuyama explains that the evolution of the universal history of humankind generates a process of homogenization: the West is the beacon and the representation of the universal values and principles, whereas the Rest resist this process of homogenization and remain trapped in problems stemming from difference and diversity:

> In the contemporary world, we see a curious double phenomenon: both the victory of the universal and homogeneous state, and the persistence of peoples. On the one hand, there is the ever-increasing homogenization of mankind being brought about by modern economics and technology, and by the spread of the idea of

rational recognition as the only legitimate basis of government around the world. On the other hand, there is everywhere a resistance to that homogenization, and a reassertion, largely on a sub-political level, of cultural identities that ultimately reinforce existing barriers between people and nations.

(Fukuyama, 1992: 244)

In the rest of the chapter, I show how the UNDP pursues these four insights in the HDRs: (1) it defends the notion that there is a (liberal) global ethics that should lead a universal global evolution; (2) it draws an identity boundary between the liberal (developed) West and the (developing) Rest; (3) it draws another identity boundary between the liberal West and other (past) Western ideologies; and (4) it prioritizes the universal, liberal global ethics over cultural diversity, and portrays the former as conflictual and dangerous. Since these insights contradict the politically correct (and allegedly plural) discourses that the UN traditionally promotes, the HDRs – especially the 2004 report – contain important discursive contradictions, which I describe and explain below.

Universal ethics and conflict

As explained above, Spencer, Parsons and Fukuyama all assume that universal ideas drive universal evolution. Their emphasis on *ideas* differentiates their conception of evolutionism from Marxism. For the former, ideas generate more advanced and evolved human societies – i.e., political liberal democracy and economical capitalism. For the latter, the material structure of societies – at the level of production and economy – causes them to change and evolve (Marx & Engels, 1968). The UNDP promotes the liberal version of evolution that ideas – rather than the clash between different groups with different interests, principles and motivations – causes societies to evolve into economic and political liberalism. In this sense, the Hegelian character of the first lines of the foreword of the 1990 HDR are very telling:

We live in stirring times. An irresistible wave of human freedom is sweeping across many lands. Not only political systems but economic structures are beginning to change in countries where democratic forces had been long suppressed. People are beginning to take charge of their own destiny in these countries. Unnecessary state interventions are on the wane. These are all reminders of *the triumph of the human spirit*.

(UNDP, 1990: iii, emphasis added)

Based on the assumption that the end of the Cold War represented the triumph of the human spirit, the UNDP asserts that 'all cultures share a commonality of basic values that are the foundation of global ethics' (UNDP, 2004: 90). Echoing both Spencer and Fukuyama, the UNDP explains that freedom and democracy are the core ideas of global culture. For example, the reports assert that 'the fight for (...) freedoms, across all cultures and races, has been the bond holding the human family together' (UNDP, 2000: 128) and that 'democracy is a universally recognized ideal, based on values common to people everywhere regardless of cultural, political, social or economic differences' (UNDP, 2002: 55). Indeed, according to the UNDP, the global liberal ethics based on a unified global culture is the key to organizing global coexistence:

> Global governance requires a common core of values, standards and attitudes, a widely felt sense of responsibility and obligations (...). The core values of respect for life, liberty, justice, equality, tolerance, mutual respect and integrity underlie the Charter of the United Nations and the Universal Declaration of Human Rights. They now need to be the guiding objectives of globalization with a human face.
>
> (UNDP, 1999: 8)

The UNDP endorses Spencer, Parsons and Fukuyama's understanding of culture – the fourth layer of the stratigraphic schema – in two ways. First, they all conflate culture with ethical values and principles. The global culture is not a set of material or practical elements, but a corpus of universal ethical values and principles that, if properly implemented, would create a peaceful coexistence for humankind. Second, they all uphold the idea that recent European history is an exemplary case of universal evolution. The UNDP perceives the Enlightenment as the central pillar for understanding and evaluating human history and evolution. The global culture based on universal ethical principles that the UNDP envisions reproduces the Enlightenment's civilization project. That is why the UNDP backs 'the Enlightenment principle that human progress will make the future look better than the past' (UNDP, 2007: 1), and finds the roots of its own institutional task – advocating policies intended to reduce inequality and promote human development – in this era:

> At the end of the eighteenth century the great thinkers of the European Enlightenment advocated ambitious social programmes

to reduce inequality and poor people's vulnerability and dependence on welfare – with a central role for public policy in financing the needed socially transformative investments. The ideas remain profoundly relevant.

(UNDP, 2005: 70)

Based on its identification with the values espoused during the Enlightenment, the UNDP constructs and articulates its implicit cultural discourse in the human development framework. The transcendental signified that sustains the discourse of the UNDP echoes the civilizational project and the principles and values of the Enlightenment. Figure 1.2 in Chapter 1 depicts universal values/conflict as the central binary opposition: the first term is privileged over the second because the Enlightenment is more present in it, while conflict represents its absence. The cultural discourse in the HDRs thus draws two identity boundaries. The first separates the West (which is privileged because it represents universal values) from the Rest (which is disadvantaged because it represents conflict). The second boundary divides the West into two fields: (1) liberalism (dominated by Enlightened values) and (2) other Western ideologies (e.g. fascism and communism) that may have some historical relationship with the Enlightenment but, according to the UNDP, betrayed that era's universal principles and resulted in totalitarian and authoritarian regimes. In other words, the West and liberalism are both implicitly linked to reason and freedom – the essential values of the Enlightenment – while the Rest and other ideologies are instead portrayed as plagued by dogma and diversity. Below, I further articulate these binary oppositions.

In this way, the UNDP's cultural discourse constructs a normative threefold division of the world – where a particularity is presented as the expression of the universal:

1   An idealized liberal West, where the universal principles of the Enlightenment thrived. While this centre is not often mentioned explicitly, it is the normalizing pattern against which the rest of the world is evaluated.
2   The Rest – countries with historical and cultural roots that are generally more distant from the Enlightenment. Since the HDRs focus on underdevelopment, they focus heavily on the Rest and link them with conflict, disorder and violence.
3   A violent West, which represents the corruption of the Enlightened principles. In these countries, the divisions are more political than

cultural. As I explain below, the HDRs sometimes mention communism as an example of inefficient management and violence; fascism and Nazism are rarely mentioned, but they are systematically used as examples of violence and intolerance within the (geographical) West.

The contradiction I analyse in this chapter emerges from this threefold division. In an attempt to demonstrate that its cultural discourse is neutral and politically correct, in the 2004 HDR the UNDP maintains that the Enlightened ethical and political principles were not exclusively Western, but form the universal and humane normative basis of every culture and religion. The report explains that *before the Enlightenment*, the West was just as intolerant and authoritarian as any other part of the world: 'Plato and Augustine were no less authoritarian in thinking than were Confucius and Kautilya'; in the 16th century 'the Inquisition was in full swing in Europe' (UNDP, 2004: 22). It also offers examples of non-Western people who promoted tolerance and respect – the Indian emperor Akbar, the Great Moghal who made pronouncements on religious tolerance in the 16th century, and the Emperor Saladin, who welcomed Maimonides to Cairo in the 12th century when he was forced to migrate from intolerant Europe. However, the report concludes that *from the Enlightenment on*, the West became a role model for the rest of the world:

> This is not to deny that tolerance and liberty are among the important achievements of modern Europe (despite some aberrations, such as brutal imperialist rules over two centuries and the Nazi atrocities six decades ago). The world indeed has much to learn from the recent history of Europe and the Western world, particularly since the period of European Enlightenment.
>
> (UNDP, 2004: 22)

The quote plainly reinforces the threefold division: (1) in the centre, an idealized Europe that represents the ideals of the Enlightenment, (2) other Westerners who did not respect the lessons of the Enlightenment and are now relegated to history, and (3) the rest of the world, which should learn from Europe. It is one of the most blatantly dislocatory statements of all 26 HDRs. By putting Europe forward as an example for the rest of the world – that is to say, to sustain the cultural discourse of the HDRs – the UNDP overlooks some of the most awful chapters of recent world history, where the real Europe was the exact opposite of this idealized conceptualization. This quote is a discursive 'volcano': the point at which all the underground tensions burst and emerge to the surface, causing disruption and jeopardizing the general solidity and legitimacy of the UNDP's discourse. However, this volcano also creates an opportunity to better understand the implicit (underground) structures and tensions underlaying the UNDP's discourse. The next section analyses these tensions.

The West and the Rest

The first identity boundary – the West vs. the Rest –parallels the historical colonizer–colonized division. Since the UNDP is part of the UN and this division is not very politically correct, the HDRs reproduce it in a very subtle – but persistent – way. The UNDP relies on the essential characteristics of the European Enlightenment (but does not explicitly mention them) to define the norm against which the Rest is discursively constructed. The Enlightenment was *modern, Western* and *white*; it championed *reason*, and was a cosmopolitan cultural, political and social movement that aimed to become *global*. The UNDP defines the characteristics of the Rest as the opposite: *traditional*, as opposed to modern; *racial*, as opposed to white; *ethnic*, as opposed to Western; *religious*, as opposed to reason; and *local*, as opposed to global. Finally, based on the assumption that the universal principles of the Enlightenment enable a peaceful, just and ordered coexistence, the Rest are portrayed as a violent, unfair, disordered and dangerous conflictual realm. A thorough reading of the HDRs shows that this discursive construction pervades the narrative. For example, the 1994 edition affirms:

> Most people derive security from their membership in a group – a family, a community, an organization, a racial or ethnic group that can provide a cultural identity and a reassuring set of values. (...) But traditional communities can also perpetuate oppressive practices: employing bonded labour and slaves and treating women particularly harshly. In Africa, hundreds of thousands of girls suffer genital mutilation each year because of the traditional practice of female circumcision. Some of these traditional practices are breaking down under the steady process of modernization.
>
> (UNDP, 1994: 31)

The quote starts by linking racial and ethnic groups with local cultural identities and values. For no apparent reason, the reflection explicitly turns to traditional groups and links them with violence and the infringement of basic rights. It then incorrectly refers to a practice that is implemented in a few countries as being performed generally 'in Africa'. Finally, the extract explains that modernization saves people from such inhuman conditions. The markers of otherness – 'race', 'ethnicity', 'tradition' and 'local' – are linked to violence, danger and conflict, while modernization is presented as their opposite. The 1999 HDR reflects on the post-Cold War period and explains:

> Local cultures have also taken on renewed vigour and significance as political movements promote local culture and local identity. In the post–cold war world local culture has often replaced ideology in politics, as the rise of fundamentalist movements reflects.
>
> (UNDP, 1999: 34)

Local cultures and identities, as opposed to the global culture envisioned by the UNDP, are directly linked to violent fundamentalist movements. The 2004 HDR echoes this link between local identities and cultures, on the one hand, and violence and fundamentalism on the other hand. This report explains that a lack of resources (poverty) causes individuals to choose religious schools that provide free education. The UNDP affirms that this is not objectionable, but that:

> In some communities such schools have also promoted coercive cultural ideologies and encouraged students to engage in coercive activities. While 2–3% of Pakistan's Islamic schools are said to be recruiting children into coercive movements, only about half the estimated 15,000–20,000 religious schools are officially registered. It becomes difficult for the state to oversee and regulate such unregistered schools. In Thailand 300 of the 550 Islamic schools offer no secular education (the state is investigating their involvement in recruiting and training militants).
>
> (UNDP, 2004: 76)

In the early 2000s, when political correctness entailed making the case that Muslims are not inherently violent, within a few lines the UNDP linked religion, Islam and terrorism based on incredibly weak facts – and in some cases based on rumour: 'Islamic schools are said to be recruiting children into coercive movements' and 'the state is investigating ...' [sic]. Rather than reporting that 97–98% of the Islamic schools in Pakistan do *not* recruit children into coercive movements, the HDR highlights the minority (2–3%) that 'are said' to do that. The paragraph following this quote recalls that 'Nazism was propagated in state schools' (UNDP, 2004: 76).

The 2013 HDR states that 'progress in human development is difficult to sustain in the face of growing or persistent inequity' and adds in an endnote: 'inequalities across racial, ethnic and religious groups are particularly likely to cause political violence and tend to be extremely persistent unless confronted by comprehensive policies' (UNDP, 2013: 87, endnote on 128). Again, the characteristics of the Rest are directly linked to violence, and the need for policies that counteract their conflictual nature. Perhaps the best example of the subtlety of the identity division between the West and the Rest is found in the very first paragraph of the 2004 HDR:

> How will the new constitution of Iraq satisfy demands for fair representation for Shiites and Kurds? Which – and how many – of the languages spoken in Afghanistan should the new constitution recognize as the official language of the state? How will the Nigerian federal court deal with a Sharia law ruling to punish adultery by death? Will the French legislature approve the proposal to ban headscarves and other religious symbols in public schools? Do Hispanics in the United States resist assimilation into the mainstream American culture? Will there be a peace accord to end fighting in Côte d'Ivoire? Will the President of Bolivia resign after mounting protests by indigenous people? Will the peace talks to end the Tamil-Sinhala conflict in Sri Lanka ever conclude? These are just some headlines from the past few months.
>
> (UNDP, 2004: 1)

At first sight, this is a normal introduction to a report focused on cultural diversity. However, what does it imply about where we find conflict, problems, instability and violence as a result of cultural diversity? The answer has three parts. First, we find conflict in the Rest (non-Western countries): Iraq, Afghanistan, Nigeria, Côte d'Ivoire, Bolivia and Sri Lanka. These conflicts are generally linked to ethnic, racial or religious issues. Second, conflict arises when people from the Rest *migrate* to the West: Muslims in France and Hispanics in the USA. Finally, there is no mention of any kind of inherently Western conflict. The West/Rest binary opposition is thus subtly reinforced: the peaceful ideal West vs. the conflictual and violent Rest.

The other Westerners

The second implicit identity division in the HDRs is between the liberal West and other ideologies that are deeply rooted in European intellectual and political history, but conflict with the UNDP's ideals. This division separates *liberalism*, which relies on the tolerant principles of the Enlightenment and, accordingly, champions reason, freedom and pluralism, from *totalitarian and authoritarian* Western ideologies – communism and Nazism – which represent the opposite (see Figure 1.2 in Chapter 1). However, in these examples, the markers of otherness in the West/Rest binary opposition do not properly work: most important examples of fascism and communism were white, Western, European, global and not based on religious beliefs. In this case, the internal division within the West is constructed under a single marker: reason. For the UNDP, fascism was not rational, and communism was not as rational (efficient) as liberalism.

In the case of communism, otherness is based on the lack of rationality and inefficient economic management. For example, the UNDP referred to the collapse of the USSR in the early 1990s with 'unnecessary state interventions (were) on the wane' (UNDP, 1990: iii). These interventions were demonstrated to be (economically) irrational and inefficient in the mid-term:

> [Former socialist] countries started with distorted economic structures. Typically, they had a high proportion of the workforce working in large enterprises with obsolete technology. And many regions had a very narrow economic base, making them very vulnerable to the play of market forces. The service sectors were generally very small and inadequate for the functioning of a modern economy. Agriculture was often very inefficient, particularly in the former Soviet Union.
>
> (UNDP, 1993: 46)

As was the case with the division between the West and the Rest, the UNDP linked communism with authoritarianism (as opposed to freedom) and totalitarian (not plural) regimes in which power derived from brutality and violence. For example:

> While socialism in the Soviet Union aspired to higher ideals, in practice it too sacrificed people, often brutally, on the altar of increased accumulation.
>
> (UNDP, 1994: 45)

> Soviet policy in Central Asia exemplified cultural intolerance. (...) the Soviet drive for rapid industrialization left little room for

cultural freedom. (...) As a result, the breakup of the Soviet Union unleashed several ethnic conflicts in its former Asian republics.

(UNDP, 1994: 62)

The otherness of fascism is described exclusively on the basis of its irrational use of violence:

> As military threats have lessened, other dangers have surfaced – such as the ethnic and religious conflicts in Bosnia, India, Iraq, Liberia, Somalia and Sri Lanka. And many industrial countries have seen violent conflicts between different racial groups – from riots in Los Angeles to neo-Nazi attacks on immigrants and asylum-seekers in Germany.
>
> (UNDP, 1993: 10)

This quote first reinforces the West/Rest divide: ethnicity and religion (markers of otherness) are linked to conflict. It then focuses on the West and highlights two kinds of violent conflicts. In both cases, the discursive structure recalls the one highlighted above (in the introduction of the 2004 report), where the conflict is related to non-Western groups living in a Western country. However, in the second case the source of violence is white, Western and European – neo-Nazis in Germany.

Similarly, in the 2004 HDR, the UNDP explains that supremacist ideologies view 'anyone who does not belong to the core community as inferior, unwanted and unworthy of respect' (UNDP, 2004: 75). The example provided from the Rest (developing countries) is Jemaah Islamiyah in Indonesia – the link between Islam and violence is reinforced. The Western examples are from the USA and Europe:

> The National Alliance – the largest neo-Nazi organization in the United States – wants to create a new government 'answerable to white people only'. Movements for cultural domination are exclusionary and seek to impose their ideology on others. They build support by engendering a sense of fear that their own values and identity are under threat. A study of extreme right parties in Europe revealed common characteristics: they foment xenophobia, leading to demands to create mono-cultural societies, to exclude 'outsiders' from welfare policies and to mould a strong state that can protect the nation from 'evil forces'. Movements of cultural domination also target members of their own community by

denigrating and suppressing dissenting opinions and questioning integrity and loyalty (purity of faith or patriotism).

(UNDP, 2004: 75)

This case displays a similar discursive pattern: the neo-Nazis are authoritarian, totalitarian and irrationally violent.

These quotes are not included to suggest, by any means, that violence should be understood differently in the HDRs or that neo-Nazism should be represented in a different way. Rather, they were selected to demonstrate that the UNDP discursively produced implicit identity boundaries that represent European liberalism as an ideal, peaceful, tolerant, rational and peaceful island in a sea of conflict and violence. These boundaries separate (1) the unstable and violent Rest from the stable and peaceful West, and (2) respectful and tolerant European liberalism from the intolerant, violent, irrational, authoritarian and totalitarian ideologies of other Westerners. Overall, the HDRs portray European liberalism as a rational and non-violent beacon that should guide the rest of the world towards a more humane stage. However, this perspective raises at least one uneasy question – which echoes Laclau's concern, at the introduction of this book, about the relation between particularism and universalism.

What about diversity?

If, as explained above, development is the process that moves humankind closer to freedom – 'the bond holding the human family together' (UNDP, 2000: 128) – and to the global ethics – 'the core values of respect for life, liberty, justice, equality, tolerance, mutual respect and integrity' that enable a globalization 'with a human face' (UNDP, 1999: 8), and if liberalism represents these values as opposed to those of the violent and conflictual others, the question then becomes: *is diversity valuable?* Under what conditions? Should we instead overcome cultural diversity and create a homogenized, peaceful, tolerant and just liberal world constructed according to the principles of the Enlightenment? How does the UNDP address the unavoidable tension between particularism (specific cultures) and universalism (global ethics) presented in the Introduction of this book?

The UNDP acknowledges this tension (UNDP, 2000: 30). The 2004 HDR directly focuses on the particular–universal relation and, echoing Fukuyama, explains that the reaction of the particular Rest to the cosmopolitan and universal values of the West is often defensive and regressive:

Struggles over identity can also lead to regressive and xenophobic policies that retard human development. They can encourage a retreat to conservatism and a rejection of change, closing off the infusion of ideas and of people who bring cosmopolitan values and the knowledge and skills that advance development.

(UNDP, 2004: 2)

The implicit content of this quote is important. The UNDP does not draw a plural map of cultural diversity and mutual influences, in which culturally equal groups influence each other. On the contrary, following an evolutionist perspective, it draws a vertical and hierarchical map where one of the poles (the West) casts positive values and principles, and the other (the Rest) rejects them. The UNDP concludes:

An extreme reaction is to shut out foreign influences, an approach that is not only xenophobic and conservative but also regressive, shrinking rather than expanding freedoms and choice.

(UNDP, 2004: 10–11)

In order to convince those who are reluctant to endorse liberal global ethics, the HDRs often insist that 'global ethics are not the imposition of "Western" values on the rest of the world. To think so would be both artificially restrictive of the scope of global ethics and an insult to other cultures, religions and communities' (UNDP, 2004: 90). Again, the implication is very telling: what if, as is most often the case, this accusation comes from other cultures, religions and communities? Are they insulting themselves? Are they necessarily regressive, conservative and xenophobic?

Seeking to properly tackle these discursive tensions, the 2004 HDR focused on the relationship between human development and cultural diversity:

States face an urgent challenge in responding to these demands (of multiculturalism). If handled well, greater recognition of identities will bring greater cultural diversity in society, enriching people's lives. But there is also a great risk. These struggles over cultural identity, if left unmanaged or managed poorly, can quickly become one of the greatest sources of instability within states and between them – and in so doing trigger conflict that takes development backwards.

(UNDP, 2004: 1–2)

It begins with a politically correct statement: cultural diversity is positive because it enriches people's lives. The report then warns that *if not
managed properly*, cultural diversity can become a source of instability
and conflict. This raises the question of what the UNDP considers the
proper management of multiculturalism. In answering this question,
the UNDP focuses on a parallel debate – individual rights vs. group
rights (UNDP, 2004: 15–16) – and avoids considering why specific,
concrete, and geographically and historically located principles and
values should be considered universal and representative of human
nature. That is to say, it ignores the tension between universalism and
particularism. However, the 2004 HDR clearly reveals the UNDP's
position on the universalism–particularism debate: it values liberty
over diversity:

> The exercise of cultural liberty may sometimes lead to a reduction
> of – rather than an increase in – cultural diversity, when people
> adapt to the lifestyles of others and choose, in a reasoned way, to
> go in that direction (unhindered by living mode exclusion). When
> that occurs, to oppose cultural liberty on the ground that it reduces
> cultural diversity would be a blunder, since liberty has con-
> stitutive – and intrinsic – importance of its own in a way that
> diversity does not.
>
> (UNDP, 2004: 23)

This quote shows that the UNDP considers liberty to have constitutive
and intrinsic value, and therefore to be more important than diversity.
In other words: 'If what is ultimately important is cultural liberty, then
the valuing of cultural diversity must take a contingent and conditional
form' (UNDP, 2004: 16). This highlights the heart of the UNDP's
cultural discourse: the freedom/diversity binary opposition, in which
freedom is privileged over diversity.

The UNDP does not further explain why freedom has intrinsic value
and diversity is secondary: the transcendental signified dogmatically
states that freedom is the essence of human beings. However, it is not a
self-evident position. The 26 HDRs do not consistently define liberty;
the closest they come is to state that freedom involves having more
choices at hand. Yet the philosophy, political science and sociology
literatures have long debated the meaning of freedom. That is to say,
there are *diverse* conceptualizations of *freedom*. Paradoxically, *diversity
forms part of a debate about freedom*. In this sense, diversity – not
sameness – is the condition of possibility of freedom. Thus, we could
also argue that diversity has intrinsic value and that a concrete

understanding of freedom is, in this sense, secondary. Then, why does the UNDP assume that freedom has intrinsic value? This question reveals the fundamental function of the transcendental signified: *if we do not assume that freedom is the essence of human beings and that it has intrinsic value, the human development framework makes no sense.* The UNDP's discourse does not hold up without an assumption that liberty has a constitutive role and diversity a contingent one. This is again paradoxical, for the UNDP's cultural discourse privileges reason over dogma (the central claim of the Enlightenment!). But to sustain its own position, it appeals to dogmatic beliefs, even when this results in contradictions, such as in the 2004 HDR:

> Justice and fairness cannot be achieved by imposing pre-conceived moral principles. Resolution of disagreements must be sought through negotiations. All parties deserve a say. *Global ethics* does not mean a single path towards peace or development or modernization. It is *a framework* within which societies can find peaceful solutions to problems.
>
> (UNDP, 2004: 90, emphasis added)

According to the UNDP's rationale, we should assume that global ethics is a neutral framework that provides an unbiased basis for fair negotiations and agreements. If all parties deserve a say, diversity should be constitutive of global ethics. However, as explained above, the UNDP implicitly limits diversity based on a normative dogmatic condition: liberalism. All the parties deserve a say *if they assume that liberty is constitutive and diversity is secondary.* Indeed, although the UNDP explains that justice and fairness cannot be achieved by imposing pre-conceived moral principles, the human development framework does exactly that. Liberalism is not a natural and neutral universal truth. On the contrary, it is a geographically and historically located moral and political construction. In the search for justice and fairness, the UNDP persists with the Victorian belief that 'the freedom of the individual, limited only by the like freedom of other individuals, *is sacred*' (Spencer, 2009: 8, emphasis added). In this way, it reproduces what Chantal Mouffe calls the paradox of liberalism:

> When a point of view is excluded it is because this is required by the exercise of reason; therefore the frontiers between what is legitimate and what is not legitimate appear as independent of power relations. Thanks to this leger-demain, rationality and

morality provide the key to solving the 'paradox of liberalism': how to eliminate its adversaries while remaining neutral.

(Mouffe, 2000: 31)

The UNDP excludes those who do not accept that liberty is constitutive and diversity is contingent. However, it argues that it does so for the sake of justice and fairness within a universal framework of global ethics. Indeed, as Mouffe points out, when the UNDP explains why liberty is more fundamental than diversity – in a quote from the 2004 report shown above – it appeals to reason: liberty can legitimately reduce diversity if it is 'in a reasoned way', although the reports do not explain what is a reasoned way to take a decision. Paradoxically, to defend liberalism over diversity, the UNDP *dogmatically* employs the central concept of the European Enlightenment – reason.

Overall, the critical analysis of the articulation of culture in the human development framework deconstructs the UNDP's discourse. The UNDP privileges reason over dogma, but dogmatically defends its position; it privileges freedom over diversity by limiting the freedom of alternative positions to take part in the debate; and it privileges universal values over conflict by privileging a particularity (the West) and portraying it as the expression of the universal. Paradoxically, the UNDP champions reason, freedom and universal values by dogmatically imposing a particular understanding of human beings.

References

Fukuyama, F. (1989) 'The End of History?', *The National Interest*, 16, 3–18.

Fukuyama, F. (1992) *The End of History and the Last Man*, New York: Free Press.

Marx, K. & F. Engels (1968) *The German Ideology*, Moscow: Progress Publishers.

Mouffe, C. (2000) *The Democratic Paradox*, London: Verso.

Spencer, H. (2009 [1862]) *First Principles*, Cambridge: Cambridge University Press.

Telleria, J. (2015) What does culture mean for the UNDP? *Cultural Studies*, 29 (2), 255–271.

UNDP (1990) *Human Development Report. Concept and Measuring of Human Development*, New York: Oxford University Press.

UNDP (1993) *Human Development Report. People's Participation*, New York: Oxford University Press.

UNDP (1994) *Human Development Report. New Dimensions of Human Security*, New York: Oxford University Press.

UNDP (1995) *Human Development Report. Gender and Human Development*, New York: Oxford University Press.

UNDP (1999) *Human Development Report. Globalization with a Human Face*, New York: Oxford University Press.

UNDP (2000) *Human Development Report. Human Rights and Human Development*, New York: Oxford University Press.

UNDP (2002) *Human Development Report. Deepening Democracy in a Fragmented World*, New York: Oxford University Press.

UNDP (2004) *Human Development Report. Cultural Liberty in Today's Diverse World*, New York: UNDP.

UNDP (2007) *Human Development Report. Fighting Climate Change: Human Solidarity in a Divided World*, New York: Palgrave Macmillan.

UNDP (2013) *Human Development Report. The Rise of the South*, New York: UNDP.

Williams, R. (1985) *Keywords. A Vocabulary of Culture and Society*, New York: Oxford University Press.

5 We are the world

> While there are robust and legitimate debates going on about the methodology and measurements we use to classify poverty, first and foremost we must remember what it actually means to be poor.
>
> (Special contribution by Melinda Gates, *Human Development Report 2016*)

Just as world hegemony transitioned from Great Britain to the USA during the 20th century, the 'Live Aid' concert that began in London on 13 July 1985 ended the same day, a few hours later, in Philadelphia (USA). This macro event was divided into two large concerts, one on each side of the Atlantic Ocean. Queen's 'We Are the Champions' (of the World) was one of the highlights in England, and the choral song 'We Are the World' that closed the concert in Philadelphia is one of the most recalled moments of the American concert. Although the lyrics of the latter sound like a nice, innocent and well-intended song – e.g., 'and the truth, you know, love is all we need' – this cultural moment was politically overloaded. It was during the Cold War: a group of Americans singing '*We are the world ... the world must come together as one ... there is a choice we are making ... we're saving our own lives ... we are the ones who'll make a brighter day ... let us realize ... that a change can only come when we stand together as one ...*' was not innocent at all. Americans were wishfully waiting for the Cold War to end so they could become the only hegemonic force in the world.

That year, 1985, Laclau and Mouffe published *Hegemony and Socialist Strategy*, in which they critically reflected on the possible political implications of the end of the Cold War. One of the most important concepts of that book was 'hegemony', which they defined as the political moment when 'a *particular* social force assumes the representation of a *totality*' (Laclau and Mouffe, 2000: x). In this sense, Americans singing 'We Are the World' – a particular group declaring that they represent the world – was what Laclau and Mouffe would consider an exemplary case of political practice. As I explain below, this political spirit subtly pervaded different influential practices that shaped our understanding of the world in the 1990s, including George H.W. Bush's invasion of Iraq, Fukuyama's proclamation of the end of history and the publication of the United Nations Development Programme (UNDP) reports analysed in this book.

Identity boundaries and the rearticulation of discourses

As explained in Chapter 1, Derrida and Laclau's post-structuralist work explains that our epistemological encounter with social reality is necessarily mediated by a discourse that constructs our understanding of the world. Since this is the only way we can access reality, this perspective implies a relational and contingent ontology, in which objects do not have a natural, positive and objective essence, but are discursively constituted. On the basis of this ontological framework, Laclau emphasizes the political dimension of discourse analysis and focuses on the discursive constitution of political identities. According to him, a political identity is constituted through an antagonistic relationship in which each side *needs* and *negates* the other. This antagonistic division enables the constitution of an identity – us, as opposed to them – and the construction of a discourse that explains reality based on the common principles, interests and objectives of the members of the group. In order to hold the group together, the discourse must conceal the internal antagonisms and contradictions that could break it up. Finally, Laclau stresses that, as the context is always evolving and changing, the discourse has to be constantly recontextualized and rearticulated to prevent the emergence of alternative identities that could jeopardize the cohesion and unity of the group.

In this chapter, I analyse the political function that the UNDP's symbolic representation of the world served between 1990 and the mid-2010s. The analysis in previous chapters shows that the UNDP plainly reproduces the two basic functions of the political game explained by Laclau. First, it constructs an identity based on an antagonistic relationship: the analysis in Chapter 4 shows that the human development reports (HDRs) construct an identity boundary between an idealized liberal, democratic, plural, modern and Western *us*, and a conflictual, problematic and violent *other*. Second, the discourse conceals the internal contradictions and potential antagonisms: the analysis in Chapter 3 explains that, although the UNDP knows that wealth is not fairly distributed – and accordingly, that the virtuous circle is not working and the inequality trap persists – the reports avoid a rigorous analysis of this problem, overlook the tensions and contradictions that capitalism generates, and continue to insist that higher levels of productivity can solve the problem.

In the following sections, I defend my argument that for almost three decades, the UNDP reproduced and promoted an understanding of the world and of global economic, political and cultural issues in a way that fitted the needs of powerful groups, which led to the formation of the status quo during the 1990s and 2000s. To do that, I first contextualize the birth of the human development framework and link it to the transition from the Cold War to the unipolar era, when the USA was the only hegemonic power in the world. I then explain that the discursive structure of the UNDP's discourse – analysed in Chapters 1 to 4 – created an antagonistic division of the world that replaced the Cold War era liberalism vs. communism antagonism. Next I show that during the 2010s, due to several changes in the international realm, the symbolic representation in the HDRs lost the ability to explain the world. Finally, I explain that we are now transitioning into a different representation of the world, based on an alternative antagonism. Although it is difficult to identify the characteristics of the new discourse at this early stage, the UN's 2030 Agenda for Sustainable Development provides useful clues. The inquiry shows that the HDRs played an important political function by rearticulating a previous understanding of the world in order to perpetuate the privileged position of the hegemonic liberal, democratic, capitalist and western *us*. In this sense, the political history of the human development framework is that of a discursive bridge that enabled the transition *from the Washington Consensus to the 2030 Agenda*.

Figure 5.1 visually represents the transitions – the discursive rearticulations – I explain in this chapter. Each section represents the antagonistic division that structured the symbolic representation of the world in each period: liberalism vs. communism during the bipolar Cold War era; development vs. underdevelopment from the early 1990s to the mid-2010s; and humankind vs. inhumanity today. This does not mean that the development–underdevelopment division did not exist before. It instead signifies that it became the central antagonism that articulated the mainstream symbolic representations of the world during the 1990s and 2000s.

Since this book focuses on the human development period, I do not analyse the evolution and rearticulation of the symbolic representation of the world during the Cold War period. Such an analysis is beyond the scope of this book. I instead describe the changes that the UNDP's

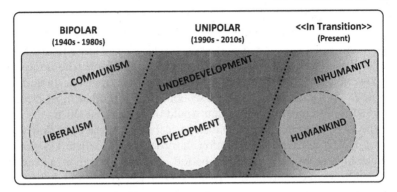

Figure 5.1 Discursive rearticulations: bipolar era, unipolar era and present

human development framework introduced in relation to previous discourses. Nor do I attempt to precisely describe the present discursive articulation: as pointed out above, I think we are transitioning into a different understanding of the world – perhaps into many different understandings – so a proper analysis is almost impossible at the moment. Only time will tell which discursive rearticulation will become more influential in the near future. I argue that the 2030 Agenda could be one such rearticulation.

When I divide this long stretch of time into three periods, I do not mean that a single discourse represented the world in each period, or that the periods are precisely defined. I simply maintain that a major antagonistic divide explains the construction of discourses during each period. For example, modernization theories, dependency theories and the Washington Consensus belong to the same period (first division in Figure 5.1), but they are diverse and in some cases contradictory. However, these theories were structured on the basis of the liberalism vs. communism antagonistic divide. While they may not have explicitly mentioned communism and capitalism, they emphasized key elements of each of these political and economic models. For instance, understanding social change, development and progress in terms of free markets vs. state intervention, *laissez-faire* vs. centralized planning, or free trade vs. regulation. In this sense, I argue that between the 1990s and the 2010s, the developed vs. underdeveloped antagonistic division replaced the liberalism vs. communism dichotomy as the central rivalry that sustained the manifold symbolic representations of the world.

Each circle in each period represents the symbolic 'us' in the liberal West during that period, whereas the term outside the circle is the symbolic representation of the menacing outside. As I explain below, it makes no sense to precisely define who is 'us' and who is 'them': these divisions are merely symbolic representations that construct identities and rhetorically evoke fears and risks. It makes more sense to ask who selected the main antagonism. In theory, it is the people who occupied a powerful position at the time of the transition from one period to another. As I explain in the next section, the group that most clearly worked to find an antagonism that would fill in the void left by the fall of the USSR on the international stage at the end of the Cold War was George H.W. Bush's administration. In order to consolidate US global leadership in the new unipolar period, his administration activated several academic, cultural and political channels that would define the new global antagonism: development vs. underdevelopment.

The birth of the human development framework

A few historical events help to contextualize the birth of the human development framework. On 9 November 1989, the Berlin Wall was opened, ending decades of division between the communist and capitalist sides of Berlin. On 2 August 1990, Iraq invaded Kuwait. On 9 September 1990, Mikhail Gorbachev and George H.W. Bush met in Helsinki. On 11 September, Bush stated in the US Congress:

> As you know, I've just returned from a very productive meeting with Soviet President Gorbachev, and I am pleased that we are working together to build a new relationship. In Helsinki, our joint statement affirmed to the world our shared resolve to counter Iraq's threat to peace. (...) Clearly, no longer can a dictator count on East–West confrontation to stymie concerted United Nations action against aggression.
>
> A new partnership of nations has begun, and we stand today at a unique and extraordinary moment. The crisis in the Persian Gulf, as grave as it is, also offers a rare opportunity to move toward an historic period of cooperation. Out of these troubled times, our fifth objective – a new world order – can emerge. A new era – freer from the threat of terror, stronger in the pursuit of justice and more secure in the quest for peace. An era in which the nations of the world, east and west, north and south, can prosper and live in harmony.[1]

The meeting in Helsinki and the invasion of Iraq were the farewell to the liberalism vs. communism dichotomy. In the quote above, Bush briefly outlined the antagonism that would define the new world order:

development vs. underdevelopment. This division pits the USA, its allies and the desire for justice and peace against dictators, terror and global instability. According to Bush, the UN would have a key articulatory function in this new era.

A few months later, on 6 March 1991, after the first Gulf War, Bush addressed the same audience and consolidated the new antagonism and the new symbolic representation of the world:

> The consequences of the conflict in the Gulf reach far beyond the confines of the Middle East. Twice before in this century, an entire world was convulsed by war. Twice this century, out of the horrors of war hope emerged for enduring peace. Twice before, those hopes proved to be a distant dream, beyond the grasp of man.
>
> Until now, the world we've known has been a world divided, a world of barbed wire and concrete block, conflict and cold war. And now, we can see a new world coming into view. A world in which there is the very real prospect of a new world order. In the words of Winston Churchill, a 'world order' in which 'the principles of justice and fair play ... protect the weak against the strong'. A world where the United Nations, freed from cold war stalemate, is poised to fulfill the historic vision of its founders. A world in which freedom and respect for human rights find a home among all nations.[2]

In order to legitimate the new symbolic representation, Bush appealed to cathartic past events that consolidated the USA's powerful position: the first and second world wars, and the birth of the UN. The new global antagonism constitutes, on the one side, the USA and the project of an ideal world of peace, respect, harmony and cooperation (akin to the UNDP's transcendental signified); on the other side is an unstable and violent world created by ruthless dictators. In this new world, the UN – 'freed from the cold war stalemate' – has a central role in achieving a 'distant dream, beyond the grasp of man'.

However, Bush's 'official' presentation of the new symbolic representation of the world in 1990–91 was the last step in a previous rearticulatory process. Between 1985 and 1988, Gorbachev and Reagan met on at least five occasions. By the late 1980s, the US administration started making dispositions for an imminent historic transition and working on rearticulating the old East–West discourse in a new updated version. As discussed in the previous chapter, Francis Fukuyama (then an official in the Policy Planning Staff of the US Department of State) published an article entitled 'The End of History?' in the influential conservative journal *The National Interest* in 1989. The Bush administration embraced Fukuyama's division between a historic and a post-historic world, in which the former relates to conflict and instability and the latter (capitalism and liberal democracies) represents peace and stability. Bush quickly understood that such a division could replace the outdated communism–capitalism antagonism. Invited by James Thompson – a former staff member of the Office of the Secretary of Defense under Gerald Ford – Fukuyama wrote the book *The End of History and the Last Man* at the RAND Corporation – the think tank created after the Second World War to offer research and analysis to the US Army (Fukuyama, 1992: ix).

The fact that the UNDP's discourse echoes Fukuyama's thesis, as shown in Chapter 4, is not a coincidence. In 1986, William H. Draper took charge as the UNDP administrator 'nominated by Ronald Reagan at the suggestion of Draper's old friend, Vice-President George H. W. Bush' (Murphy, 2006: 234). Draper spent most of his professional life in venture capital until Reagan appointed him to serve as the president and chairman of the US Export-Import Bank in 1981, where he stayed until he took over the UNDP (Browne, 2011: 36). According to Murphy, a well-known historian of the UNDP, Draper was a straightforward, enthusiastic American businessman, dedicated and passionate about the private sector, who had 'no abiding interest in strengthening Third World governments' (Murphy, 2006: 234). Murphy explains that in 1989, 'it was easy to believe that the Programme's glory days were over' because other organizations 'had begun to eclipse UNDP in its traditional fields' (Murphy, 2006: 232). However, Murphy and Browne agree that Draper transformed the organization and gave it a new lease on life by adopting *advocacy* as one of its main tasks in 1989 (Browne, 2011: 48; Murphy, 2006: 240). That year, Draper contacted Mahbub ul Haq, a former World Bank economist, and invited him to lead the project of preparing an annual report that would 'give the organization a new, globally significant, purpose' (Murphy, 2006: 233). Indeed, it was 'significant' and 'global': the UNDP's new advocacy task would consist of *globally promoting a re-signification of the world* – i.e., a new symbolic representation of it. The first HDR was published in May 1990. In the Preface, Draper – echoing Fukuyama's Hegelian understanding of history – described the end of the Cold War as 'the triumph of the human spirit' (UNDP, 1990: iii). Draper reproduced Bush's second speech to Congress in the Preface of the 1991 HDR:

> The 1990s began with a great surge of hope. (...) A new era of human rights and political freedom seemed to be dawning. These

hopes were brutally dashed when Iraq invaded Kuwait. But the world by then was already a new world – a world free of the East-West divide. The international community, through the United Nations, joined force to condemn and repulse the aggression. (...) Development needs peace. The framework for strengthened international cooperation in support of global security exists in the United Nations. It can provide the platform for member states to build a new world – a world of peace and development (...).

Human Development Report 1991 holds a mirror to the world events of the past year. It is about the sensible reallocation of resources to serve humanity better by involving as many people as possible in the creative use of those resources rather than only a few vested interests. It is about participatory development where people are placed at the centre of all decision-making. It is about human freedom where the creative energies of the people are unleashed to generate economic and social opportunities for themselves and for their societies. And it is about the process of human development whose main aim is to develop and use all human capabilities.

(UNDP, 1991: iii)

The new representation of the world was ready: outside, underdevelopment and those who destabilize the world; inside, the UN and a project of peace and development. In this new stage, human development was the way to face the new global antagonism: development vs. underdevelopment.

The key elements of the rearticulation

During the 1990s, the UNDP worked to adapt the human development framework laid out in the HDRs to the new symbolic representation of the world. I identify five important changes in the new discourse. Two of them correspond to the general changes in social sciences during the 1990s, when the critical drive in development studies shifted from Marxist and Neo-Marxist approaches to a Foucauldian post-structuralist perspective (Nederveen, 2001: 10–17). The first change is a shift in focus from the macro to the micro level. Although the UNDP continued to measure development at the country level – for example in the Human Development Index (HDI) – and to reflect in terms of country strategies and policies – such as the publication of national HDRs since 1992 – the new discourse turned the spotlight on the people. As mentioned several times throughout the book, the new development paradigm put people at the centre of the debate, sought to make them not only the means to, but also the end of social change, and in general aimed to ensure that 'development cooperation focuse(d) directly on people, not just on nation-states' (Draper in UNDP, 1993: iii).

Second, the UNDP's new discourse moved from a purely quantitative to a more qualitative approach. For example, based on the assumption that qualitative aspects were important for the measurement of development, the UNDP added health and education to the measurement of income to calculate the HDI. These two shifts provided an adequate basis for elaborating on the identity boundaries analysed in Chapter 4. The new antagonism was not interpellating individuals as citizens of a country – i.e., you are Russian, therefore communist; you are American, therefore capitalist – but as potential members of a global community based on shared values – i.e., no matter where you are, if you embrace these common values, you are one of *us* who strive for human development and, therefore, for a better world. The country-based logic shifted to a subjectivity- and identity-based one.[3]

However, the three most distinctive novelties in the UNDP's discourse responded to the need to adapt it to the new representation of the world. First, as explained in Chapter 4, *the UNDP reinforced the idea of an antagonistic underdeveloped other – outside the identity boundary – that threatens the existence of the peaceful community inside it.* After the communist threat ended, the UNDP profusely insisted in the 1990s that the new threat to peace, security and stability was poverty and underdevelopment. In other words, the UNDP described horrid problems for the stability of the world – war, terrorism, massive migration, environmental degradation, etc. – that were systematically linked to underdevelopment and poverty. The message was clear: 'global poverty is one of the greatest threats to the sustainability of the physical environment and to the sustainability *of human life*' (UNDP, 1992: 2, emphasis added). This message pervades the early reports:

> This new human order would recognize that we are all one community on an increasingly crowded planet. This interdependence implies more than economic links. Environmental threats respect no national boundaries – and *poverty is the driving force* behind many of them. Nor can the international peace process be limited to that between East and West – violence can erupt in any part of the world and affect us all. And how can 80% of the world's people be denied the resource they need without inviting unprecedented waves of international migration?
>
> (UNDP, 1991: 78–79, emphasis added)

The 1994 HDR was key in this respect. The first paragraph of the report explained that the origin of future conflicts was 'buried deep in growing socio-economic deprivation and disparities', and concluded:

> The search for security in such a milieu *lies in development, not in arms.* More generally, it will not be possible for the community of nations to achieve any of its major goals – not peace, not environmental protection, not human rights or democratization, not fertility reduction, not social integration – except in the context of sustainable development that leads to human security
>
> (UNDP, 1994: 1, emphasis added)

The 1994 report linked security to development – and therefore, *under*development to *in*security. To reinforce this rationale, it precisely described the antagonistic 'outside':

> The threats to human security are no longer just personal or local or national. They are becoming global: with drugs, AIDS, terrorism, pollution, nuclear proliferation. Global poverty and environmental problems respect no national border. Their grim consequences travel the world. (...) The same speed that has helped unify the world has also brought many problems to our doorsteps with devastating suddenness.
>
> (UNDP, 1994: 2)

There is a very important aspect of this specific rearticulation of the antagonistic divide. In the previous period, capitalism was confronted by a rival political and economic project – communism. Moreover, the ideological basis of both projects was rooted in the noble principles of the European Enlightenment: both capitalism and communism allegedly sought an ideal future in which people would be free and live in dignity. In the new symbolic representation of the world, the liberal West was not confronted by an adversarial rational economic and political project. On the contrary, underdevelopment was related to a lack of efficiency, mismanagement and the unacceptable interests of dangerous dictators. In the UNDP's representation, on the other side of the antagonistic boundary we find humans (as in the case of communism) but not a political and economic rational project: just barbaric and cruel people and the problems they generate – poverty, hunger, war, terrorism, migrations, environmental degradation, drugs, lack of human rights and democracy, etc. The new representation of the world was highly depoliticized: development was not represented as a matter of political decisions, but instead as driven by common sense, morality and rational choices. The new division was not markets vs. the state, but rather good vs. evil.

The expression 'bring problems to our doorsteps' in the quote above vividly evokes the idea of a traditionally peaceful and stable community invaded by foreign issues, which takes us to the second key element of the discursive transformation in the early 1990s. In the human development discourse, *the world is portrayed as a group of people with the potential to become a single, unified and homogeneous community in peace and harmony.* However, the discursive construction of this community is submitted to a twofold logic. On the one hand, the UNDP stresses the elements that make every individual and every human group the same – what Laclau calls 'the logic of equivalence' (Laclau, 2005: 70, 77). Indeed, as explained in Chapters 1 and 2, the human development framework relies on the fundamental idea that we all share a common essence that makes all of us equal: humans. For example:

> We are a global community in every sense. Not just economically interdependent, but sharing a common environment – and exposed to common risks of war and social dislocation. Consider the damage that will be done if we do not fully accept this. Global trade and economic growth will suffer. The environment will be further degraded. Wars will break out to settle unresolved tensions. Millions deprived of economic opportunity will migrate in search of a better life. A global compact for human development should be based on the recognition of the need for a new *human* order.
> (UNDP, 1991: 10–11, emphasis added)

Alongside the global community, the UNDP also reinforces the idea of a common menace: We are one because we all share the same threats.

On the other hand, the other implicit logic stresses the aspects that make individuals and human groups different – what Laclau calls 'the logic of difference' (Laclau, 2005: 77, 79). In some cases, the differential logic is clear. For instance, Chapter 4 discusses the UNDP's construction of a boundary between the peaceful West and the conflictual Rest. In other cases, this logic is very subtle. For example: 'the world cannot be made safe without the full collaboration of all – rich and poor, North and South. Only through cooperation can the world achieve sustainable human development' (UNDP, 1992: 9). The reports stress that although we are a single community, there are differences within this community: rich and poor, North and South, developed and developing, and so on. These distinctions echo Derrida's binary oppositions outlined in Chapter 1, and how one of the terms is privileged on the basis of the transcendental signified.

This interaction of equivalential and differential logics makes the boundary between the peaceful inside and the dangerous outside difficult to define. It is more an abstract idea than a line. Those who share some abstract and allegedly universal principles – peace, cooperation, respect, coexistence and so on – are, or might be, members of the global community. Those who do not share these principles – a symbolic violent and conflictual Rest, exemplified by Saddam Hussein – are not part of the community. The UNDP does not describe the boundary precisely, but offers a rough, quantitative and country-based proxy: the HDI. Those at the top of the annually published list of countries ranked according to the HDI tend to be part of the global community; those in the middle and below are closer to the source of the key problems – poverty and underdevelopment.

Antagonisms and the empty signifier

The third key distinctive element of the discursive rearticulation is how the global community – inside the antagonistic divide – is presented. *The new discourse represents the symbolic inside as free of internal contradictions and antagonisms.* Here I analyse two examples of how the discourse constructs such a representation. First, as pointed out at the end of Chapter 3, the UNDP does not mention capitalism. This term could pit members of the inside – for example, those who think the state should play an important role in development strategies – against those with a more liberal perspective. So the UNDP uses it very few times, and generally to refer to the past. Sometimes it is used to review the evolution of economic theory and the birth of industrial societies during the last two centuries – in Chapter 2 of the 1996 HDR, for example – and at other times to recall the period when capitalism and communism struggled:

> So far, the basic motivation for donors to give aid has been to win friends in the cold-war confrontation between socialism and capitalism. (...) The changed circumstances of the 1990s demand an entirely new approach to ODA.
>
> (UNDP, 1993: 7)

In any case, the term 'capitalism' is seldom used in the reports; when it is used, it systematically lacks an explanatory function in relation to current development issues – for example in explaining the inequality trap, as pointed out in Chapter 3 in this book. It is very telling that, in the 2019 HDR, which is focused on inequalities, the word capitalism is used only once: in an endnote on page 259, to briefly mention that Piketty and Zucman (2014) and Kuznets (1955) have divergent opinions on the relationship between economic growth and distribution. That is all: no further analysis of the link between capitalism and distribution, just two bibliographical references in small type at the end of the report.

The second example is the depolitization of development issues explained above. In the UNDP's discourse, the development–underdevelopment antagonism has no political connotations. For the UNDP, development is not a matter of choosing between different basic principles and alternatives. As explained in Chapters 2, 3 and 4, the human development framework implicitly imposes these basic principles – a specific anthropological and sociological understanding of human beings and a set of political assumptions – and portrays development exclusively as a matter of properly managing the resources to advance towards the ideal horizon defined by the transcendental signified. Such a technical understanding of poverty, exclusion and discrimination reduces the chances that antagonistic political positions will emerge among those who promote human development. A good example is the use of the term 'governance'. It does not refer to inherently political decisions about the future we want and the principles that should guide decisions about how to organize coexistence. As Horkheimer explained (Chapter 3 in this book), in a competitive environment where markets are the institution that articulates coexistence, the only goal is productivity and efficiency; governance is what Foucault described as governmentality: a matter of avoiding disturbances and properly channelling people's energy in an efficient way (Foucault, 1990: 133–159). The early reports provide several examples of this managerial understanding of political issues. However, the clearest examples come from the 1999 HDR, which focused on how to govern globalization:

> None of these pernicious trends – growing marginalization, growing human insecurity, growing inequality – is inevitable. With political will and commitment in the global community, they can all be reversed. With stronger governance – local, national, regional and global – the benefits of competitive markets can be preserved with clear rules and boundaries, and stronger action can be taken to meet the needs of human development. Governance does

not mean mere government. It means the framework of rules, institutions and established practices that *set limits and give incentives for the behaviour of individuals, organizations and firms.* Without strong governance, the dangers of global conflicts could be a reality of the 21st century.

(UNDP, 1999: 7–8, emphasis added)

The first interesting aspect of this quote is that governance is presented as a practice undertaken by the community (inside) that keeps at bay the threats of the dangerous outside: the 21st century could be horrible – marginalization, insecurity, inequality – if the UNDP's message is not understood. The second is that, although the UNDP champions democracy – the political system in which confrontations between alternative views on political issues are resolved through the participation of the people – the quote shows that in the new discourse, democracy is reduced to governance: an allegedly apolitical practice that maximizes the benefits of competitive markets by channelling the conduct of the people. Politics and democracy are reduced to a liberal management of society. From this perspective, governance does not allow room for dissension and internal antagonisms: a peaceful 21st century requires competitive markets and good management of the behaviour of the people.

As explained in Chapter 1, Laclau says that the key notion that makes such a complex discursive articulation possible – a threatening outside vs. a peaceful inside free of antagonisms and submitted to both equivalential and differential logics – is an empty signifier. It is a term that represents the highest aspirations of the community, highlights the equivalential logics, insinuates the differential logics, and constantly points to the menacing outside. It must be empty and evocative enough to keep the (inherently diverse and potentially antagonistic) community together. In the UNDP's representation of the world, this term is 'human development'. It simultaneously points to the external threat (underdevelopment), highlights the equivalential element (human) and insinuates the differential aspect (development: some countries are developed, others are developing). This signifier is abstract enough not to imply any political and economic commitment. It points far into the ideal horizon defined by the transcendental signified, and at the same time describes (the absence of) development – through the HDI, for example. The proof that this term functions very well as an empty signifier is that, in the HDRs, the UNDP gathers 'special contributions' – brief pieces of text signed by well-known individuals who are not UNDP staff – from very diverse people who probably have different (even antagonistic) political views. Previous HDRs have contained contributions from Ted Turner (American businessman, founder of CNN), Ole Henrik Magga (chairman of the UN Permanent Forum on Indigenous Issues), Hillary Clinton (former Secretary of State, senator and first lady of the USA), Hamid Karzai (former president of the Transitional Islamic State of Afghanistan), Gordon Brown (former prime minister of the UK), Olafur Eliasson (artist and activist), Bill and Melinda Gates (co-chairs of the Bill & Melinda Gates Foundation), Juan Manuel Santos (president of Colombia and 2016 Nobel Peace Prize Laureate), Mirna Cunningham Kain (Nicaraguan Miskitu and indigenous peoples rights activist), and Angela Merkel (German chancellor), among others. And in the elaboration of the national HDRs – more than 700 since 1992 – the UNDP implements participatory techniques designed to collect the voices of poor and excluded people. All of them – Ted Turner, Hillary Clinton, Bill Gates and excluded people alike – agree that 'human development' *is the solution.*

The death of the human development framework

The great success of the rearticulated discourse that adapted to the new context in the 1990s was that almost everyone ended up understanding the world through the discourse promoted by Bush, Fukuyama and the UNDP. In development debates, the human development framework became the humanist fortress in the fight against the radically capitalistic and neoliberal proposals of the Washington Consensus adherents. For two decades, this discourse had a pleasant and successful life: most people involved in development issues respected and praised it as an example of a slightly progressive approach to global issues. The UNDP's discourse became the banner that many admirers of the positive aspects of communism and socialism in the previous period ended up accepting in their confrontation against the development strategies promoted by the International Monetary Fund and the World Bank. The communism vs. capitalism antagonism was tamed, reconstructed, reduced and internalized in liberal, capitalist harmless terms: human development vs. Washington Consensus.

However, in the early to mid-2010s, some important international events caused the foundations of the UNDP's discourse to tremble and fall. I analyse three of these here. The first was the global financial crisis that began in 2007 and unfolded during the first half of the 2010s. This crisis showed that the problems that the UNDP's discourse traditionally presented as issues from the undeveloped outside – such as the economic and financial crises in Latin America, Africa and Asia between the 1970s and the 2000s – were now a reality in the liberal, developed, democratic West.

> The recent global financial crisis and the East Asian financial crisis of 1997–1998 remind us that progress is not linear, *even for countries that perform well*. Economic crises can throw countries off track.
>
> (UNDP, 2010: 30, emphasis added)

During the crisis, the elected democratic governments of Italy and Greece, for example, were temporally replaced by unelected technocrats. When the democratically elected government of Greece organized an official referendum to decide on the country's future, international capital did not accept the result and imposed measures that the people had democratically rejected. The crisis showed that the liberal and democratic West was not a peaceful and stable backwater; on the contrary, it was inhabited by profound antagonisms and contradictions. It also demonstrated that the developed–underdeveloped boundary was no longer meaningful because the problems of the antagonistic outside were now part of the inside, and that democracy and participation were not inherent elements of the coexistence within the ideal global community, but a suspendable instrument that is hierarchically submitted to the logics of capitalism.

The second event was the UK's vote in 2016 to leave the European Union (EU). The results of the referendum, the polarization of British (and European) societies, and the ensuing tough and endless negotiations between Great Britain and the EU confirmed some of the insights discussed above. The universalistic idealizations of the UNDP's discourse, and the belief in the existence of a global culture that can unite humankind in the pursuit of a better future – analysed in Chapters 2 and 4 – were called into question. The 'Brexit' vote problematized the UNDP's essentialist assumptions and showed that the world is an antagonistic field in which different groups of people – with different principles, motivations, interests and objectives – struggle to implement their political projects. It also exemplified that the construction of identity boundaries not only separates people along the development–underdevelopment antagonistic divide. On the contrary, Brexit demonstrated that identities could divide people ... even in the cradle of liberalism!

> At a time when global action and collaboration are imperative, self-identities are narrowing. Social and political movements linked

to identity, whether nationalist or ethnopolitical, seem to be increasing in frequency and strength. Identity politics are on the rise. Data from 1816 to 2001 show a peak in 2001 when almost 90 percent of the conflicts in the world were being fought by nationalists seeking to establish separate nation-states or between ethnicities over ethnic balances of power within existing states. The Brexit is one of the most recent examples of a retreat to nationalism among individuals who are feeling alienated in a changing world. This shift towards support for nationalism might have been foreseen.

(UNDP, 2016: 81)

Moreover, this antagonistic and conflictual division was democratically organized by a democratically elected government in a democratic country, and resolved through a democratic referendum. The quote above shows that, for the UNDP, democratic processes are positive if the result concurs with the alleged universal ethics – otherwise they should be 'foreseen'. As in the case of the financial crisis, this event demonstrated that the problems of the underdeveloped outside were part of the developed inside too; that the idealized West was as antagonistic as the Rest; and that identity tensions could emerge even within democratic, liberal developed countries.

The final event, and perhaps the most relevant to the UNDP's focus, was China's emergence as a major international figure. The impressive rise of its economy and the success of its fight against poverty during the 2000s and 2010s – which lessened the impact of the failure of the Millennium Development Goals – shook the foundations of the UNDP's discourse. During the financial crisis, the tables were turned and the members of the discursive outside became exemplary:

During these uncertain times, countries of the South are collectively bolstering world economic growth, lifting other developing economies, reducing poverty and increasing wealth on a grand scale. They still face formidable challenges and are home to many of the world's poor. But they have demonstrated how pragmatic policies and a strong focus on human development can release the opportunities latent in their economies, facilitated by globalization.

(UNDP, 2013: 1)

In this quote, the UNDP emphasizes the strong focus on human development of countries like China. However, in reality, China's case problematized the basic assumptions of the human development discourse: a non-democratic and politically communist country ruled by a single party was now an example in the fight against poverty and of successful development strategies. Indeed, the UNDP had to invent a new term to speak positively about China in the 2013 without mentioning single-party communism: proactive developmental state.

> A strong, proactive and responsible (developmental) state develops policies for both public and private sectors – based on a long-term vision and leadership, shared norms and values, and rules and institutions that build trust and cohesion.
>
> (UNDP, 2013: 4)

In the 2013 report, the UNDP praised *long-term* vision and *leadership* (sic) and forgot about democracy and participation. Overall, the identity boundaries of the UNDP's discourse were not useful to describe the world anymore; the peaceful and stable inside of the development–underdevelopment antagonism was not the ideal backwater that Bush envisioned in 1990; and the conflictual and unstable outside was exemplary in many regards. The symbolic representation constructed in 1990 no longer applied to the world of the 2010s.

In transition

It is very difficult to outline the new antagonism and the new discursive articulation that will replace the development–underdevelopment discourse because the transition is happening right now, and it is difficult to write the history of the present. Moreover, the extraordinary events that have recently shaken the world – this book was partially written during 8 weeks of confinement due to COVID-19 – make it even more difficult to gauge the global balance of power, and to ascertain whether a transition is underway to a multipolar or an apolar world, or any other kind of restructuration of power relations. Accordingly, it is difficult to know if a single symbolic representation of the world will be hegemonic in the future, or, on the contrary, many different views will coexist.

With the information at hand at this moment, it seems that the UN is working on a new rearticulation of the previous hegemonic discourse based on a new antagonistic division, which can be found in the 2030 Agenda for Sustainable Development, published in 2015. I find three important aspects suggesting that the 2030 Agenda is an important element of this rearticulation. First, in the 2030 Agenda, the interior of the antagonistic division changes a little. The equivalential logic – what makes the members equal – remains the same: it stresses that human-kind is a single collective group:

> We are setting out *together* on the path towards sustainable development, devoting ourselves *collectively* to the pursuit of global development and of 'win-win' cooperation which can bring huge gains to *all countries and all parts of the world.*
>
> (UN, 2015: paragraph 18, emphasis added)

Indeed, the document is entitled 'Transforming *our* world', and the text is written exclusively using the first-person plural: we/us (Telleria, 2018). However, there is an interesting change regarding the differential logics – what makes the members different. The 2030 Agenda downplays the developed–developing (North–South) division:

> [The 2030 Agenda for Sustainable Development] is an Agenda of unprecedented scope and significance. It is accepted by all countries and is applicable to all (...). These are universal goals and targets which involve the entire world, developed and developing countries alike.
>
> (UN, 2015: paragraph 5)

In contrast to the Millennium Declaration of 2000, which stressed the traditional North–South divide – akin to the UNDP's discourse – the 2030 Agenda interpellates developed and developing countries alike. Many praised this novelty as a sign of a more egalitarian understanding of global issues. Based on the analysis in this book, I understand it as a sign that capitalism has achieved a stage at which it imposes the same problems – with different levels of intensity – on all of humankind. The problems that affected the underdeveloped outside in the 1990s and 2000s – financial crises, identity conflicts, unelected imposed technocratic governments, epidemics, and so on – are now global and affect developed and developing countries alike.

The second important shift relates to the horrid outside on the other side of the antagonistic divide. It still features poverty; a lack of dignity; inequalities; disparities in opportunity, wealth and power; gender inequality; unemployment; global health threats; natural disasters; spiralling conflicts; violent extremisms and terrorism; humanitarian crises and forced displacement; environmental degradation, desertification, freshwater scarcity and loss of biodiversity; and so on (UN, 2015: paragraph 14). However, in the new representation, some global threats gain visibility – such as natural disasters, viruses and health threats, and climate change – and are presented as detached from human agency. ·As many analysts have pointed out (e.g., Bexell & Jönsson, 2017; Gabay & Ilcan, 2017; Mediavilla & García-Arias, 2019; Soederberg, 2017; Suliman, 2017; Telleria, 2018, 2020b; Weber, 2017), the agenda does not focus on the political, social or economic causes of the problems it allegedly aims to solve:

> A systematic flaw in the Agenda's approach is the lack of analysis. It does not look into the underlying causes for the state of the world. There is no political economy approach to understanding the genesis and cycles of poverty and inequities. The agenda is oblivious to power relations (...).
>
> (Koehler, 2016: 152)

In the UNDP's discourse, on the other side of the antagonistic divide we find human agency: dictators, religious fanatics, terrorists, fundamentalists, adherents of radical ideologies, and so on. In the language of the 2030 Agenda, problems just happen and have to be solved. The agenda blames no one, which is a further step in the technification and depoliticization of global problems.

Finally, and based on the previous two aspects, the 2030 Agenda constructs a new global antagonism: humankind vs. inhumanity. According to the new rhetoric, only if we accomplish the agenda's objectives will we overcome 'the challenges which humanity faces' (UN, 2015: paragraph 14) and reach our 'full human potential' (UN, 2015: paragraph 20). The agenda describes an ideal future as a world free of poverty, hunger, disease, fear and violence; where physical, mental and social wellbeing are assured; where food is sufficient, safe, affordable and nutritious; where there is universal access to affordable, reliable and sustainable energy; with universal respect for human rights and human dignity, the rule of law, justice, equality and non-discrimination; with respect for race, ethnicity and cultural diversity; in which humanity lives in harmony with nature and in which wildlife and other living species are protected (UN, 2015: paragraphs 7, 8 and 9). The 2030 Agenda is the project of the entire humankind, which leaves no one behind in the pursuit of an ideal, perfect future world. Such a project is presented as the only way to avoid the inhumane, horrid problems that threaten humankind as a whole.

In this sense, the Millennium Development Goals (MDGs) represent a parallel way that coexisted during the 2000s and early 2010s with the human development framework and, at the same time, opened the way to the 2030 Agenda. The MDGs share some of the characteristics of the UNDP's discourse – the transcendental signified that points far towards an ideal horizon, and the differential division between North and South – and some of the characteristics of the 2030 Agenda – they are a global compound, signed by every country and passed by the UN General Assembly, that unites and coordinates several organizations and UN bodies, not just a single programme. Indeed, five discursive elements suggest that the 2030 Agenda does not represent a break with the UNDP's discourse, but instead a rearticulation based on a different antagonistic divide. More precisely, these five aspects show that the agenda could be an attempt by the international figures who led the status quo during the 1990s and 2000s to keep mainstream discourses under control up to 2030, in a world that is transitioning to a new stage. These five discursive elements are (Telleria 2018, 2020b):

1   The 2030 Agenda seeks legitimacy from the same source that Bush did in 1991: the end of the Second World War and the creation of the UN. That is to say, the world order in which the USA and capitalism occupied a hegemonic global position during the 1990s and 2000s. The agenda explains:

Seventy years ago, an earlier generation of world leaders came together to create the United Nations. From the ashes of war and division they fashioned this Organization and the values of peace, dialogue and international cooperation which underpin it. The supreme embodiment of those values is the Charter of the United Nations. Today we are also taking a decision of great historic significance. (…) 'We the Peoples' are the celebrated opening words of the UN Charter. It is 'We the Peoples' who are embarking today on the road to 2030.

(UN, 2015: paragraphs 49, 50 and 52)

2   The 2030 Agenda uses the same style to promote a new symbolic representation of the world as the UNDP did in 1990: a humanist project to take the world to an ideal stage, led by the UN.
3   Such an ideal stage is based on the same transcendental signified as used by the UNDP: the assumption that there exists a human essence that, if properly understood and developed, will result in ideal individuals who will create an ideal world.
4   The 2030 Agenda advances the process of depoliticization of global issues started by the UNDP: in the liberalism vs. communism antagonism, the outside was represented by a political and

economic project; in the period of the development vs. under-development antagonism, the other side of the divide was characterized by irrational projects led by evil people (dictators, terrorists, fanatics); finally, in the world representation based on the humankind vs. inhumanity antagonistic divide, the 2030 Agenda mentions no one on the other side of the antagonistic divide, just non-anthropogenic problems that threaten the existence of humankind.

5   Finally, Laclau explains that equivalential logics are stressed, at the expense of differential ones, when the leading group feels that its privileged position is being questioned (Laclau & Mouffe, 1985: 113–120). The fact that the 2030 Agenda lessens the differential logics could be understood as a sign that the group leading the world economically, politically and militarily during the 1990s and 2000s understands that the international economic, financial, military and political events of the 2010s jeopardize its hegemonic position.

However, as pointed out above, it is too early to extract solid conclusions about the transition from one symbolic representation of the world to another. In a few years we will have the time/distance and the information to ascertain what is happening during the current transition.

Notes

1 Speech by US President George H.W. Bush to a joint session of the US Congress, Washington, DC, 11 September 1990.
2 Speech by US President George H.W. Bush, to a joint session of the US Congress, Washington, DC, on 6 March 1991.
3 For an analysis of how the UNDP's discourse constitutes subjectivities, see Telleria 2020a.

References

Bexell, M. & K. Jönsson (2017) Responsibility and the United Nations' Sustainable Development Goals, *Forum for Development Studies*, 44 (1), 13–29.

Browne, S. (2011) *The UN Development Programme and System*, Abingdon: Routledge.

Foucault, M. (1990) *The History of Sexuality, Volume 1: An Introduction*, New York: Vintage.

Fukuyama, F. (1992) *The End of History and the Last Man*, New York: Free Press.

Gabay, C. & S. Ilcan (2017) Leaving no-one behind? The politics of destination in the 2030 Sustainable Development Goals, *Globalizations*, 14 (3), 337–342.

Koehler, G. (2016) Assessing the SDGs from the standpoint of eco-social policy: using the SDGs subversively, *Journal of International and Comparative Social Policy*, 32 (2), 149–164.

Kuznets, S. (1955) Economic growth and income inequality, *American Economic Review*, 45 (1), 1–28.

Laclau, E. (2005) *On Populist Reason*, London: Verso.

Laclau, E. & C. Mouffe (1985) *Hegemony and Socialist Strategy*, London: Verso.

Laclau, E. & C. Mouffe (2000) *Hegemony and Socialist Strategy*, London: Verso (2nd edn).

Mediavilla, J. & J. García-Arias (2019) Philanthrocapitalism as a neoliberal (development agenda) artefact: philanthropic discourse and hegemony in (financing for) international development, *Globalizations*, 16 (6), 857–875.

Murphy, C. (2006) *The United Nations Development Programme: A Better Way?*Cambridge: Cambridge University Press.

Nederveen, J. (2001) *Development Theory: Deconstructions/Reconstructions*, London: Sage.

Piketty, T. & G. Zucman (2014) Capital is back: wealth–income ratios in rich countries 1700–2010, *Quarterly Journal of Economics*, 129 (3), 1155–1210.

Telleria, J. (2018) Can we 'transform our world' without affecting international power relations? A political analysis of the United Nations development agenda, *Globalizations*, 15 (5), 655–669.

Telleria, J. (2020a) Development and participation: whose participation? A critical analysis of the UNDP's participatory research methods, *European Journal of Development Research*, published online 29 May 2020.

Telleria, J. (2020b) Policies without politics: the exclusion of power dynamics in the construction of 'sustainable development', in G. Koehler, A.D. Cimadamore, F. Kiwan & P.M.M. Gonzalez (eds), *The Politics of Social Inclusion: Bridging Knowledge and Policies Towards Social Change*, Paris: UNESCO/CROP/Ibidem Press, pp. 99–114.

Soederberg, S. (2017) Universal access to affordable housing? Interrogating an elusive Development Goal, *Globalizations*, 14 (3), 343–359.

Suliman, S. (2017) Migration and development after 2015, *Globalizations*, 14 (3), 415–431.

UN (2015) *Transforming Our World: The 2030 Agenda for Sustainable Development*. Resolution A/RES/70/1, adopted by the General Assembly on 25 September 2015. New York: United Nations.

UNDP (1990) *Human Development Report. Concept and Measuring of Human Development*, New York: Oxford University Press.

UNDP (1991) *Human Development Report. Financing Human Development*, New York: Oxford University Press.

UNDP (1992) *Human Development Report. Global Dimensions of Human Development*, New York: Oxford University Press.

UNDP (1993) *Human Development Report. Peoples' Participation*, New York: Oxford University Press.

UNDP (1994) *Human Development Report. New Dimensions of Human Security*, New York: Oxford University Press.

UNDP (1999) *Human Development Report. Globalization with a Human Face*, New York: Oxford University Press.

UNDP (2010) *The Real Wealth of Nations: Pathways to Human Development*, New York: Palgrave Macmillan.

UNDP (2013) *Human Development Report. The Rise of the South*, New York: UNDP.

UNDP (2016) *Human Development Report. Human Development for Everyone*, New York: UNDP.

Weber, H. (2017) Politics of 'leaving no one behind': contesting the 2030 Sustainable Development Goals agenda, *Globalizations*, 14 (3), 399–414.

Conclusion
Past, ____ and future

Main elements of the UNDP's discourse

The inquiry in this book started with the question *what are the onto-logical assumptions in the symbolic representation of the world constructed by the UNDP in the HDRs, and what are their political consequences?* The following quote summarizes the findings of the analysis in Chapters 1–5:

> Modernity started with the aspiration to a limitless historical actor, who would be able to ensure the fullness of a perfectly instituted social order. Whatever the road leading to that fullness (...) it always implied that the agents of that historical transformation would be able to overcome all particularism and all limitation and bring about a society reconciled with itself. That is what, for modernity, true universality meant.
>
> (Laclau, 1996: 51)

Three elements in this quote describe the key characteristics of the UNDP's discourse. The first is the conviction that fulfilling a perfectly instituted social order is the end of history and human evolution. As explained in Chapter 1, the UNDP's discourse is sustained by the unquestioned 19th-century assumption that freedom is the essence of human beings. The assumption is that the proper unfolding of this essence will result in healthy, rational, intelligent and skilful individuals who will form a peaceful, harmonious and stable society, free of essential contradictions. On the basis of this essentialist ontology, the UNDP constructs the internal logic of its discourse: a stratigraphic and individualistic conceptualization of human beings and society (Chapter 2); a theorization of human development as the activation of the virtuous circle that empowers people (Chapter 3); and an evolutionist explanation of history in which the liberal West is located at the tip of the arrow of human evolution (Chapter 4).

The second element is the idea that a limitless historical actor could lead the way to such a perfectly instituted social order. The UNDP's discourse relies on the idea that the liberal West is the incarnation of such a historical actor. During the Cold War, the identity of this historical actor was constituted through the liberalism vs. communism antagonism; after the Cold War, its identity was rearticulated around the development vs. underdevelopment antagonism (Chapter 5). To construct such a symbolic representation of the world, the HDRs conceal the inherent contradictions of the capitalist West and construct a horrid and dangerous 'outside' that threatens the stability of the world, and even the existence of humankind – in other words, it jeopardizes the evolution towards the perfectly instituted social order.

The third element is the metaphor of the road that stretches from particularism to universalism. In the UNDP's discourse, that is the idea of human development – the unfolding of the human essence. The concept of human development contributes an implicit evolutionist representation of time, which divides history into three symbolic sections. First, the past, where the ideal universalism and the material and conflictual particularism remain distant. Within this representation, only Western culture – *the privileged agent of history*, to use Laclau's expression – mediates between the particularity of the people and the universality of the humanist principles and values of the Enlightenment. Second, the future, which is envisioned as the yet-to-come moment when the material reality of the world and the ideal values of the Enlightenment merge: it is the realization of an ideal, harmonious, peaceful, just, sustainable and stable society in which the essence of human beings is fully unfolded. Third, in between the past and the future is *a paradoxical present, which does not exist as such.* In the HDRs, the present does not have meaning and value for its own sake: it is the mere transition between the corrupted material past and the ideal realization of universal values and principles. In other words, in the UNDP's discourse the present is only meaningful in contrast to the past to overcome (underdevelopment) and the future yet to come (the absolute unfolding of human essence). That is why the Human Development Index ranks countries between two symbolic moments: the corrupted and conflictual past (0) and the future yet-to-come (1). Chapter 1 points out that for the UNDP, democracy and human development are more a journey and a promise than a destination. That is also why the UNDP rarely uses the word 'capitalism' in its reports – because they do not describe the present political and economic dynamics that sustain the status quo, or the existing power structures that explain the increasing inequality.

Rethinking human development?

A symbolic representation of history that avoids the present as such and explains it exclusively in terms of the past and future encounters a crisis when the present – the one that is being concealed – changes. That is why, as explained in Chapter 5, the UNDP's discourse faltered during the 2010s: the present became too obvious to be concealed. The UNDP is aware of this crisis. In 2020 – while this book was being written – the UNDP and the International Science Council started a discussion entitled 'Rethinking Human Development'.[1] The organizers explained that, due to several ecological, health, political and economic crises, the time has come 'to rearticulate Human Development for the 21st century'.

Six aspects suggest that the outcome of this discussion will be an updated version of the present-less discourse of the last three decades. First, the project remains faithful to the 19th-century individualistic and essentialist conceptualization of human beings and society. Although it describes humans as social beings and focuses on the 'collective and relational dimensions' of human development, in doing so, it reproduces the essentialist ontology in which (1) the individual is assumed to have an essence that ontologically precedes the constitution of society; (2) society is conceptualized as the set of surrounding institutions that, if properly articulated, create the right environment for the human essence to thrive (that is why people's 'wellbeing is dependent on social institutions that allow them to flourish'); and (3) conflict and violence are understood as alien to human nature and 'remain fundamental threats' to the proper unfolding of such an essence. In other words, the theorization of social issues remains trapped in the essentialist and ahistorical ontological moment in which virtual individuals constitute society:

> Without compromising the principle that human beings are entitled to rights or are endowed with individual choice and capabilities, human development needs to capture the key role that collective relationships, norms and identities, and institutions have in achieving human development.

Within this ontological framework, relations systematically have a secondary position: *first*, the individual is fully constituted, *then* relations, institutions, social interactions and political identities arise.

Second, the project remains faithful to the stratigraphic schema, in which individuals must adapt to the changing environment to self-preserve and survive – that is why healthy individuals need 'physiological resilience (...) to deal with change and continue to develop'.

Third, the project assumes that the human development framework – a particular understanding of social change and human agency, which draws on the anthropological assumptions of 19th-century evolutionist sociology – belongs to the realm of universal values and principles. Accordingly, it explains that since 'human societies are also grounded in spatiotemporal histories' – the realm of particularism – the universal human development framework 'need(s) to take into account local (or national and regional) specificities' and 'include space for recognition of these factors and consideration of locally relevant responses'.

Fourth, the project reproduces the symbolic menacing 'outside' that threatens the stability – and even the existence – of humankind. On the one hand, the menacing outside is described following the perspective explained in Chapter 4: it comprises the risks and threats from the Rest and menacing the West – e.g., '9/11 and international terrorism at the beginning of the 21st century; the SARS epidemic in *Asia* in 2002/03, the Ebola crisis in *Africa* in 2014/16; *Syrian* refugees and *African* citizens *moving towards Europe* in 2015/16; the COVID-19 pandemic in 2020' (emphasis added). On the other hand, it reinforces the depoliticizing tendency explained in Chapter 5: specific global issues that menace humankind are presented as events that just happen, devoid of any agency or intention – e.g., 'the global financial crisis in 2008/09; the climate crisis and other dynamics of global environmental change as a *threat to human civilization*' (emphasis added).

Fifth, although the project mentions the relational nature of contemporary societies, it does not discuss capitalism or focus on current power relations, or the economic and political dynamics that generate inequality, poverty and discrimination. In other words, only people with irrational and unmoral behaviour, viruses and climate change threaten humankind – not the political and economic dynamics implemented by powerful people with vested interests. That is why progress is seen as a process of enlarging people's choices and well-being, as well as enhancing individual capabilities, which happens in a kind of political, economic and social vacuum.

Finally, the project explains that 'the world around us evolves', but does not reflect on whether the international organization created in the 1940s by Franklin D. Roosevelt (USA) and Winston Churchill (UK), with the approval of Joseph Stalin (USSR), remains the best institutional frame to deal with 21st-century global issues: it just assumes that it is.

Final thoughts: constructing a relational approach to social issues

The question remains: how to construct a relational approach to social issues? As discussed in Chapter 1, Derrida explains that deconstruction is not a demolition, after which we find only dust and useless debris. On the contrary, it opens up a plural space where the pieces of the deconstructed building enable the construction of alternative approaches to the present. In other words, deconstruction reactivates sedimented assumptions and allows different symbolic representations of the world and of history to emerge. It does not take us closer to the truth, for that would be contrary to the post-structuralist perspective. The merit of deconstruction is that it forces us to accept our located and partial existence, and introduces room for plurality. For that reason, constructing an alternative explanation of the present is not a methodological issue, but a matter of changing the ontological assumptions that sustain the current approach to reality. It requires redefining the relationship between particularism and universalism, where the latter is assumed to be a special case of the former – a particularity powerful enough to present itself as universal.

A relational perspective on social issues requires an ontology that explains the present in terms of power relations. The following five aspects help to construct a relational approach to social issues:

1 *Ontological and epistemological bearings.* A relational approach implies that the observer (the subject) is part of the observed (the object). Hence, his existence is embedded in the historical power dynamics that led up to the present. From this perspective, a transparent (unmediated) approach to reality is impossible. Accordingly, any understanding of reality is necessarily mediated by a discourse – that is to say, by a historically constituted symbolic representation that makes reality meaningful.

2 *Past and future.* A relational approach to social issues implies accepting that any representation of the past and future is merely a discursive construction intended to explain and legitimize the present. This does not mean that a relational approach to reality focuses exclusively on the present, for any symbolic representation of the world requires an explanation of the past and some expectations about the future. A relational perspective requires that these representations of the past and future are not conceptualized

as the privileged expression of a universal truth, but as one symbolic representation of the world *among many*.

3   *Present*. The previous aspects suggest a new understanding of the present as the political realm in which different groups with plural, alternative and legitimate symbolic representations of the world struggle to implement their political project according to their principles, interests, motivations and objectives. According to this understanding of the present, there is no universal human essence that enables a consensus that benefits all. On the contrary, each group may have a different understanding of human beings and social coexistence. Hence, conflict (not violence) is constitutive of social life and is therefore ineradicable. For that reason, analysing the present requires explaining the power relations that sustain the status quo as well as the hegemonic symbolic representation of the world and of history.

4   *Development*. Within this new relational realm, development logics are systematically deconstructed. In a plural and conflictual realm, there is not a single universal understanding of human beings, nor an ideal non-conflictual future in which human essence perfectly unfolds – in other words, the endless quest for fullness and perfection disappears. A relational approach to social issues does not explain history as the unfolding of the human essence and the evolution to a perfect stage. On the contrary, it explains history as the always-changing coexistence of different representations of the world – a constant evolution from one structure of power relations to another. The more the different groups are ready to accept plurality, and the more skilled they are at finding temporal agreements, the more peaceful the process would be.

5   *Inequality and power*. A relational approach implies accepting that the benefit of some groups often happens at the expense of others. According to this perspective, inequality and the lack of distribution are not mysteries that just happen, but the result of specific decisions that benefit some at the expense of others. In this sense, a relational approach does not conceptualize global issues as the result of a lack of development, or as unintended (apolitical) threats to the existence of humankind – viruses, climate change, etc. Rather, it explains global issues as the result of specific decisions taken within a structure of power relations. From this perspective, the best way to fathom a global issue is to ask – *who benefits from this problem*?

Since fear is the essential instrument of domination, the relational approach to reality described above opens up opportunities for emancipation. According to this approach, there is no universal 'outside' that menaces the existence of humankind. On the contrary, there are different powerful groups taking decisions that benefit some at the expense of others. In this sense, security is not a matter of struggling against a menacing outside that threatens humankind. Instead, it entails explaining that the only menace to humankind in the 21st century is a world led by people who assume that their truth is the universal truth. This book seeks to demonstrate that the menace to humankind is not outside, but inside.

Note

1 https://council.science/human-development/ [All the quotes in this subsection were extracted from this website]

Reference

Laclau, E. (1996) *Emancipation(s)*, London: Verso.

Index

Printed in the United States
by Baker & Taylor Publisher Services